Summer Bridge Activities™ *for Young Christians*

Fourth Grade to Fifth Grade

SBA was created by
Michele D. Van Leeuwen

written by
Julia Ann Hobbs
Carla Dawn Fisher
Sabena Maiden

exercise illustrations by
Amanda Sorensen
Magen Mitchell

This Book Contains...

- Fun, skill-based activities in **reading, writing, arithmetic,** and **language arts** with additional activities in **geography** and **science** to keep your child busy, happy, and learning! *Summer Bridge Activities™ for Young Christians* is divided into three sections for review and preview with pages numbered by day. Children complete their work quickly with the easy-to-use format, leaving lots of time for play!

- A **Reading Book List** based on the Accelerated Reader Program and classic Christian titles.

- **Motivational Calendar** to encourage summer learning and reward your child's efforts. **"Discover Something New"** lists of creative things to do are found on the back of each *Summer Bridge Activities™ for Young Christians* Motivational Calendar for when your child says the inevitable: "What can I do? I'm bored."

- Comprehensive **Word Lists**, which contain words to sound, read, and spell, challenge children and encourage them to build their vocabulary. *Summer Bridge Activities™ for Young Christians* 4–5 also contains **Division and Multiplication Flashcards.**

- **Tear-out answer pages** to help correct your child's work.

- An official **Certificate of Completion** to be awarded for successfully completing the workbook.

Here are some groups who think our books are great!

YOUTH EDUCATION EXCELLENCE 1993-99

Hey Kids and Parents!
Log on to
www.SummerBridgeActivities.com
for more eye-boggling, mind-bending, brain-twisting summer fun...
It's where summer brains
like you hang out!

Summer Bridge Activities™ for Young Christians
4th Grade to 5th Grade

RBP thanks those involved in the creation of this book:

Andy Carlson, Russ Flint, Robyn Funk, Kristina Kugler, Carol Layton,
Magen Mitchell, Paul Rawlins, Amanda Sorensen, George Starks

Please visit our website at
www.summerbridgeactivities.com
for supplements, additions, and corrections to this book.

First Edition 2006

ISBN: 1-59441-712-1

PRINTED IN THE UNITED STATES OF AMERICA
10 9 8 7 6 5 4 3 2 1

Table of Contents

Dear Parents,

Thank you for choosing Summer Bridge Activities™ for Young Christians to help reinforce your children's classroom skills while away from school. This year, we are proud to offer you this unique edition, which contains ways to help your children develop their minds and further their Christian walk this summer. This book is full of skill-building activities to reinforce the valuable academics that your children need, coupled with exercises and ideas to foster their Christian growth.

Family is the foundation of life. That is why it is imperative that you work with your children to help them be the best they can be—the best Christians, the best students, the best citizens. As parents, you must instill core values that will stay with your children throughout their lives. We created this book to assist you, as a parent, as you foster your child's academic and spiritual development. Inside, you will find helpful introductory material with valuable resources and ideas for building your child's Christian character, including a book list containing classic children's literature along with Christian resources to further strengthen your child's mind and spirit. This section is followed by ten weeks of daily, age-appropriate academic activities. The book wraps up with a bonus Bible Camp Section. The activities in the bonus section are intended to be completed alongside daily academic skill reinforcement.

This book is different from other skill-building books, for while its obvious goal is to build and maintain academic skills over the summer, it also encourages your children to enhance their spiritual skills as well. At the beginning of each day, you and your children are encouraged to complete a short daily devotional to help get them focused not only on the task before them but also to start the entire day in the right frame of mind—on God. The daily devotionals are made up of Bible verses and quotes that foster a positive character and a Christian attitude.

We hope that you and your children get the most out of Summer Bridge Activities™ for Young Christians. May God bless you as you strive to help your children build a strong bridge to success in the classroom and in life!

Sincerely,

Michele D. Van Leeuwen

Sabena Maiden

Ms. Hansen TAKES YOU INSIDE

Summer Bridge Activities™

for Young Christians

The exercises that are found in **Summer Bridge Activities™** for Young Christians (SBAYC) are easy to understand and are presented in a way that allows your child to review familiar skills and then be progressively challenged on more difficult subjects. In addition to academic exercises, SBAYC contains many other activities to challenge and reinforce your children's knowledge of the Bible and further develop their Christian walk with God.

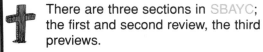

Sections of SBAYC

✝ There are three sections in SBAYC; the first and second review, the third previews.

✝ Each section begins with an SBAYC Motivational Calendar.

✝ Each day your child will complete an activity in reading, writing, arithmetic, and language skills. The activities progressively become more challenging.

✝ Each page is numbered by day. Have your child start the day by reading the daily devotional.

✝ Your child will need a pencil, ruler, eraser, and crayons to complete the activities.

Books Children Love to Read

📖 SBAYC contains a Reading Book List with a variety of titles, including many that are found in the Accelerated Reader Program. In addition, you will find many quality books by Christian authors. Christian resources are noted with a †.

📖 We recommend that parents read to their pre-kindergarten through 1st grade children 5 to 10 minutes each day and then ask questions about the story to reinforce comprehension. For higher grade levels, we recommend the following daily reading times: grades 1–2, 10 to 20 minutes; grades 2–3, 20 to 30 minutes; grades 3–4, 30 to 45 minutes; grades 4–5 and 5–6, 45 to 60 minutes.

📖 It is important that the parent and child decide an amount of reading time and write it on the SBAYC Motivational Calendar.

SBAYC Motivational Calendars

🖍 Calendars are located at the beginning of each section.

🖍 We suggest that the parent and child sign the SBAYC Motivational Calendar before the child begins each section.

🖍 When your child completes one day of SBAYC, he/she may color or initial the star.

🖍 Refer to the recommended reading times. When your child completes the agreed reading time each day, he/she may color or initial the book.

🖍 The parent may also initial the SBAYC Motivational Calendar once the activities have been completed.

🖍 We recommend completing the daily devotional and marking it on the calendar before doing the academic exercises so your child begins the day's activities focused and ready.

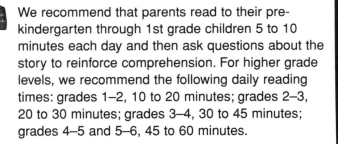

10 Helpful Hints on How to Maximize your child's character.

 1 Read the Bible with your children every day. Point out specific examples of how God recognizes those who show good character.

 2 Be a good example to your children. Exhibit the behaviors and standards that you want to see them use. Sometimes children can learn more from what you do than what you say.

 3 With your children, define what good character means to your family. Identify specific traits, such as respect and honesty, that you want your family to strive for.

 4 Make a Family Character Chart. When a family member displays good character, indicate it on the chart with a sticker or check mark. Build in a special family incentive, such as a special family dinner or trip, for when a family goal has been reached.

 5 Recognize when someone in the family has displayed good Christian character. Mention it in front of the entire family at dinner or some other time when the family is together. Acknowledging positive examples presents a clear message that good character is important in your family (and recognizing good character may have a contagious effect).

 6 Post your family's values for all to see. This may be done by posting a list of the house rules and goals on the refrigerator, or it may be a mission statement cross-stitched and hung in a frame. Make it simple enough so that even your youngest child will understand your family's values.

 7 Make fun character craft projects and activities to serve as friendly reminders, particularly when certain family values are not being remembered. These can be fun, simple ideas, such as a mobile that lists each Christian character trait that your family has agreed upon or cookies with kind words to each other written in icing.

 8 Provide your children with positive role models through quality resources. There are many books, magazines, youth organizations, music concerts, websites, videos, and DVDs that promote good values and character. Make them available to your children.

 9 Encourage your children to be charitable. There are many ways that your family can get involved with helping others. Whether you volunteer regularly at a soup kitchen or have a monthly family collection of used clothes, toys, and other household items to give to a local charity, show your children how much helping others enriches everyone's lives. This will also provide numerous "hands-on" opportunities for strengthening character.

 10 Talk to your children and listen to them as they share their thoughts, ideas, and opinions. An important part of establishing your family's good values begins with your children feeling valued themselves.

 **"Love Never Fails"** (1 Corinthians 13:4–8)

The Bible speaks a great deal about God's love for us. **1 John 4:8** even tells us that "God is love." And because God loves each of us so much, we, too, should share that incredible gift with others. The way to show Christian character is to display love in our daily actions. God provides us the ultimate example of Christian character that each person should strive for. **Exodus 34:6–7** refers to God as "The LORD, the LORD, the compassionate and gracious God, slow to anger, abounding in love and faithfulness, maintaining love to thousands, and forgiving wickedness, rebellion and sin."

Use this checklist with your family as a daily reminder of how they can exemplify Christian character through loving actions.

Today I can show my best Christian character by...

- being patient with others, even when it is difficult.
  Love is patient,

- showing kindness to others.
  love is kind.

  ♡God is love.♡

- being content with the things that I have.
  It does not envy,

- using kind, encouraging words when I speak.
  it does not boast,

- being respectful and not showing off.
  it is not proud.

- showing a positive attitude.
  It is not rude,

- looking to see how I can help others, not just myself.
  it is not selfseeking,

- being calm and not using anger in a hurtful way.
  it is not easily angered,

- forgiving others and not holding grudges.
  it keeps no record of wrongs.

- doing activities that please the Lord.
  Love does not delight in evil but rejoices with the truth.

Encourage Your Child To Read The Bible

 Make fun games based on your family's favorite board games or game shows. Prepare questions and answers based on biblical facts, and use the rules from the original game. This is a great activity for family game night.

 Help your children learn the books of the Bible in order using a fun, made-up tune or familiar song.

 Conduct family "Sword Drills." Call out a specific chapter and verse reference, and see who can find it first to read to the family. This is a great way for your children to learn the order of the books in the Bible.

 Familiarize your children with Scripture by making a Bible treasure hunt. Pose questions to your children that will require them to search through the scriptures for the answers.

 Buy your child a study Bible specific to his or her age and reading level.

 Regularly tell your children stories from Scripture. No child is too young to listen to a bedtime story or hear an interesting true tale while in the car. Share a Bible story with your children either from memory or use a good Bible storybook. (There are many wonderful Christian resources available in print and on the Web.)

 Read the Bible with your children. Make it a daily habit to share a special verse at breakfast or before going to bed.

 Read your Bible. Let your children see you enjoying the Word of God daily. Also, share specific things from your reading that your children can benefit from and understand.

Reading Book List

† Indicates Christian Resource

Atwater, Richard
Mr. Popper's Penguins

Ballard, Robert D.
Finding the Titanic

Berger, Barbara
Gwinna

Blume, Judy
Tales of a Fourth Grade Nothing

Brammer, Deb
Peanut Butter Friends in a Chop Suey World †

Brink, Carol Ryrie
Caddie Woodlawn

Cleary, Beverly
Emily's Runaway Imagination
The Mouse and the Motorcycle
Socks

Clifford, Eth
Help! I'm a Prisoner in the Library

Cole, Joanna
The Magic School Bus books

Coville, Bruce
My Teacher Is an Alien

Dahl, Roald
Charlie and the Chocolate Factory
Charlie and the Great Glass Elevator
Fantastic Mr. Fox
George's Marvelous Medicine
Matilda

DaVoll, Barbara
Midnight Madness and Mayhem †

Dixon, Franklin W.
Hardy Boys mysteries

Doyle, Arthur Conan, Sir
Sherlock Holmes mysteries

Estes, Eleanor Ruth
The Hundred Dresses

Farley, Walter
The Black Stallion

Fendler, Donn and Joseph B. Egan
Lost on a Mountain in Maine †

Ferguson, Alane
Cricket and the Crackerbox Kid

Fitzgerald, John Dennis
The Great Brain books

Fleischman, Sid
The Whipping Boy

Gardiner, John R.
Stone Fox

Giff, Patricia R.
Fourth Grade Celebrity

Grove, Vicki
Good-Bye, My Wishing Star

Hass, E. A.
Incognito Mosquito
Incognito Mosquito Flies Again
Incognito Mosquito, Private Insective

Henderson, Dee
Uncommon Heroes Series †

Howat, Irene
Ten Boys Who Made a Difference †
Ten Girls Who Changed the World †

Hunkin, Oliver
Dangerous Journey †

Keene, Carolyn
Nancy Drew mysteries

Kingfisher Publications
1,000 Facts about People
1,000 Facts about Earth
1,000 Facts about Wild Animals
Forest Animals
Freshwater Animals
Polar Animals

King-Smith, Dick
Babe: The Gallant Pig
The Fox Busters
Martin's Mice

Kline, Suzy
Orp
Orp and the Chop Suey Burgers
Orp Goes to the Hoop

Lawson, Robert
Rabbit Hill

L'Engle, Madeleine
The Glorious Impossible †

Lenski, Lois
Strawberry Girl

Leppard, Lois Gladys
Mandie and the Secret Tunnel †

Lewis, C.S.
The Chronicles of Narnia †

Lowry, Lois
All about Sam
Anastasia Krupnik Series
Attaboy, Sam!

Lucado, Max
The Children of the King †

MacDonald, Kate
The Anne of Green Gables Cookbook

MacLachlan, Patricia
Sarah, Plain and Tall

Manes, Stephanie
Chocolate Covered Ants
Maselli, Chris
Shut Down! †
Double-Take †
Mills, Lauren A.
The Rag Coat
Morey, Walt
Gentle Ben
Kävik, the Wolf Dog
Mowat, Farley
Owls in the Family
Myers, Bill
My Life as a Smashed Burrito †
Naylor, Phyllis Reynolds
Shiloh
Osborne, Rick
Bible Heroes and Bad Guys †
Paulsen, Gary
Dunc and Amos Hit the Big Top
Hatchet
Rodomonte's Revenge
The Wild Culpepper Cruise
Peet, Bill
Bill Peet: An Autobiography
Prelutsky, Jack
For Laughing Out Loud:
Poems to Tickle Your Funnybone
Pryor, Bonnie
Poison Ivy and Eyebrow Wigs
Richards, Lawrence O.
It Couldn't Just Happen †
Richardson, Arleta
In Grandma's Attic †
Richler, Mordecia
Jacob Two-Two Meets the Hooded Fang
Rockwell, Thomas
How to Eat Fried Worms
Rue, Nancy
The Chicago Years Series †

Sacajawea Books

Hogrogian, Nonny
Sacajawea
Jassem, Kate
Sacajawea: Wilderness Guide
Ingoglia, Gina
Sacajawea and the Journey to the Pacific
O'Dell, Scott
Streams to the River, River to the Sea
Sachar, Louis
There's a Boy in the Girls' Bathroom
Sideways Stories from Wayside School
Schulz, Charles
For the Love of Peanuts
Scieszka, Jon
The Good, the Bad, and the Goofy
Knights of the Kitchen Table
Silverstein, Shel
Where the Sidewalk Ends
Smouse, Phil
God Is in the Small Stuff †
St. John, Patricia
Treasures of the Snow †
Twice Freed †
Taylor, Kenneth N.
Everything a Child Should Know About God †
Taylor, Paul S.
The Great Dinosaur Mystery and the Bible †
Titus, Eve
Basil of Baker Street

Usborne Science Activities

Science in the Kitchen
Science with Air
Science with Batteries
Science with Light and Mirrors
Science with Magnets
Science with Plants
Science with Weather
Wilkinson, Bruce
Secrets of the Vine for Kids †
The Adventure Bible (NIV) †
Wittman, Sally
Stepbrother Sabotage

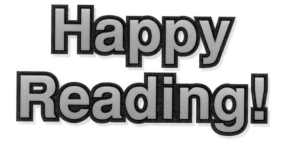

Motivational Calendar!

Month _____

My parents and I decided that if I complete 15 days of
Summer Bridge Activities™ for Young Christians and
read _____ minutes a day, my incentive/reward will be:

_____

Child's Signature _____ Parent's Signature _____

Day 1 ☆ 🕊 📖 _____   Day 9 ☆ 🕊 📖 _____

Day 2 ☆ 🕊 📖 _____   Day 10 ☆ 🕊 📖 _____

Day 3 ☆ 🕊 📖 _____   Day 11 ☆ 🕊 📖 _____

Day 4 ☆ 🕊 📖 _____   Day 12 ☆ 🕊 📖 _____

Day 5 ☆ 🕊 📖 _____   Day 13 ☆ 🕊 📖 _____

Day 6 ☆ 🕊 📖 _____   Day 14 ☆ 🕊 📖 _____

Day 7 ☆ 🕊 📖 _____   Day 15 ☆ 🕊 📖 _____

Day 8 ☆ 🕊 📖 _____

Child: Color the ☆ for daily activities completed.
Color the 🕊 for daily devotionals completed.
Color the 📖 for daily reading completed.
Parent: Initial the ____ when all activities are complete.

Jesus loves me!

Fun Activity Ideas to Go Along with the First Section!

1. Describe what you look like and write it down.

2. Make a picnic lunch for two; then invite a friend over and have a picnic in your backyard.

3. Feed the birds.

4. Ask your mom or dad for an old map and plan a trip. Decide on a destination and highlight your route. Figure out how many days it would take, where you would stop, and what you would like to see. Use the legend on the map to help you make these decisions.

5. Find some old socks, buttons, yarn, and needle and thread. Make puppets and name them. Then find a cardboard box and paint it. Cut a hole in the front to put the puppets through and put on a puppet show for younger children.

6. Polish a pair of your mom's or dad's shoes and put a love note in the toe.

7. Visit a sick neighbor, friend, or relative.

8. Hold a fire drill in your home.

9. Start a diary.

10. Learn how to do something you have always wanted to do, like play the guitar, cross-stitch, rollerblade, cook pizza, train your dog, etc.

11. Write a story about your friend.

12. In the evening, look at the sky. Look at the amazing world God made for you. Say a prayer of thanks to God.

13. Pick one of your favorite foods and learn how to make it.

14. Have a watermelon bust.

15. Make a pitcher of lemonade or tropical Kool-Aid and sell it in front of your house.

Mixed Skills Practice.
Watch the operation signs.

Romans 5:5
And hope does not dis-
appoint us, because
God has poured out
his love into our hearts
by the Holy Spirit…

Day 1

1. $13 - 5 =$ _8_
2. $17 - 9 =$ _8_
3. $0 \div 3 =$ _0_
4. $3 \times 6 =$ _18_
5. $6 + 4 =$ _10_
6. $20 \div 4 =$ _5_
7. $9 + 2 =$ _11_
8. $1 \times 2 =$ _2_

9. $10 \div 2 =$ _5_
10. $4 \times 3 =$ _12_
11. $13 + 5 =$ _18_
12. $6 - 0 =$ _6_
13. $6 \times 5 =$ _29_
14. $15 - 9 =$ _6_
15. $30 \div 6 =$ _5_
16. $6 + 9 =$ _16_

17. $27 \div 3 =$ _9_
18. $9 \times 7 =$ _63_
19. $7 + 9 =$ _16_
20. $25 \div 5 =$ _5_
21. $12 - 4 =$ _8_
22. $8 + 5 =$ _13_
23. $13 - 6 =$ _7_

Find the missing number.

24. $18 \div \boxed{3} = 6$
25. $5 + \boxed{1} = 6$
26. $10 - \boxed{7} = 3$
27. $24 \div \boxed{8} = 3$

28. $\boxed{2} \div 4 = 8$
29. $3 \times \boxed{7} = 21$
30. $\boxed{24} \div 6 = 4$
31. $\boxed{5} + 4 = 9$

32. $\boxed{6} + 6 = 12$
33. $4 \times \boxed{9} = 36$
34. $\boxed{13} - 6 = 7$
35. $\boxed{0} \times 7 = 0$

36. $11 - \boxed{9} = 2$
37. $\boxed{} \times 8 = 8$
38. $10 - \boxed{} = 8$
39. $4 + \boxed{} = 12$

• •

Write <u>yes</u> before each group of words that make a sentence. Write <u>no</u> if the group is not a sentence. (<u>Remember</u>: A sentence is a group of words that express a complete thought.)

_____ **1.** Tom carried the canned food.

_____ **2.** Butterflies have beautiful.

_____ **3.** For his tenth birthday.

_____ **4.** Turtles have hard shells.

_____ **5.** Everyone enjoyed the trip.

_____ **6.** Have you fastened?

_____ **7.** Wash your hands before.

_____ **8.** Will you feed the pets?

_____ **9.** Don't forget to call me.

_____ **10.** Prayed for her.

_____ **11.** We will turn to page.

_____ **12.** Ants are insects.

_____ **13.** Do you have hiking boots?

_____ **14.** Cats are furry.

_____ **15.** Mark likes to go swimming.

_____ **16.** Our green tent.

Food comes in various containers. Write what foods might come in the following containers (or be packaged a certain way). Then list containers of your own.

Your List

A bag of

A bucket of

A box of

A bottle of

A carton of

A glass of

A pan of

A can of

A jar of

A tube of

A cube of

A bar of

Seek and Find. The telephone book is a reference book. There is a lot of useful information in a telephone book.

The **White Pages** list people's names and telephone numbers in alphabetical order by last name.

The **Yellow Pages** list businesses' telephone numbers by type of business. Emergency information is in the front of the book.

1. Find a friend's name and number in the telephone book and write them down.

   _____

2. Look up and list the phone numbers that would be helpful to you in case of an emergency. _____

   _____

   _____

3. Find your school's phone number. _____

4. Look up your favorite restaurant's phone number. _____

5. Look up the phone numbers of your favorite places to go. _____

   _____

   _____

6. Look up the phone numbers of workplaces of people you know. _____

   _____

Add or subtract these 3- or 4-digit numbers.

Day 2

1. 681
   + 145

2. 569
   − 247

3. 3,744
   − 1,378

4. 248
   + 48

5. 143
   + 219

6. 2,830
   − 519

7. 9,873
   + 828

8. 5,893
   + 3,072

9. 304
   − 172

10. 4,918
   + 3,928

11. 6,219
   − 4,356

12. 2,456
   + 1,529

13. 1,375
   + 6,518

14. 428
   − 119

15. 2,709
   + 1,282

16. 7,645
   − 564

17. 1,680
   − 354

18. 6,142
   − 2,525

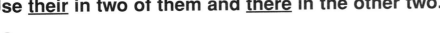

Add the correct word—their or there. Remember: their means "they own" or "have," and there means "in or at the place," or it can begin a sentence.

1. _____ must be something wrong with that cow.
2. The Hills were training _____ horse to jump.
3. We are going to _____ farm tomorrow.
4. Please put the boxes over _____.
5. _____ will be sixteen people at the party.
6. Will you please sit here, not _____?
7. _____ barn burned down yesterday.
8. They will put _____ animals in Mr. Jack's barn tonight.

Write four sentences about your church.
Use their in two of them and there in the other two.

9. _____

10. _____

11. _____

12. _____

Suffixes. A suffix is a syllable added to the end of a base word.
Add the suffix in the middle of the suffix wheel to the end of the base word.
Write the new word. Remember: You may need to double the final consonant
or change a y to an i when adding a suffix.

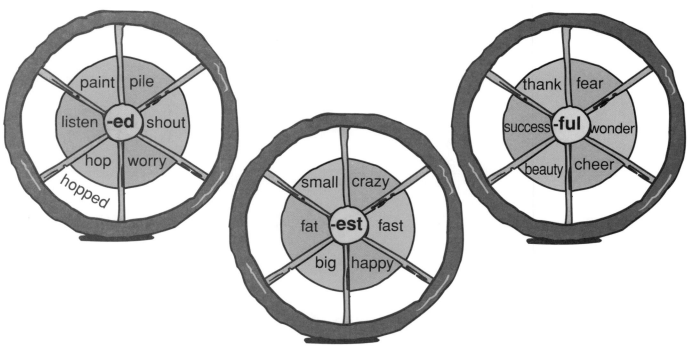

Producers and Consumers. Write answers to the following questions or discuss them with an adult.

1. Name some producers. _____
   _____

2. How are producers and consumers different?_____
   _____
   _____

3. What do profit, labor, and wages have to do with producers and consumers?
   _____

4. How are producers and consumers interdependent? _____
   _____
   _____

5. Must people buy what they need or want from other people? _____
   _____

6. How do you think consumers and producers of today are different from consumers and producers of years ago? _____
   _____
   _____

Understanding Thousands.
Write each number in standard form.

Romans 8:25
But if we hope for what
we do not yet have,
we wait for it patiently.

Day
3

1. 8 thousands, 3 tens,
   9 ones
   8,039
   _____

2. 6,000 + 300 + 10 + 2
   _____

3. 3 thousands, 8 hun-
   dreds, 4 tens, 1 one
   _____

4. 5,000 + 700 + 3
   _____

5. 7 thousands,
   1 hundred, 7 ones
   _____

6. 9,000 + 900 + 90 + 9
   _____

7. 2 thousands,
   9 hundreds,
   6 tens, 2 ones
   _____

8. 1,000 + 8
   _____

9. 1 thousand, 7 tens,
   5 ones
   _____

10. 2,000 + 900 + 80 + 9
    _____

11. 6 thousands,
    9 hundreds, 9 tens,
    6 ones
    _____

12. 1,000 + 400 + 10
    _____

13. 0 thousands,
    4 hundreds, 7 tens
    _____

14. 7,000 + 900 + 5
    _____

15. 4 thousands, 5 tens
    _____

16. 3,000 + 10 + 5
    _____

Read the following paragraph and answer the questions.

Kangaroos are furry, hopping mammals that live only in Australia. Antelope kangaroos live on the plains in the north. Gray kangaroos live mostly in the grasslands and forests of eastern and southern Australia. Red kangaroos make their home in the deserts and dry grasslands in the central part of the country, and most wallaroos live in dry, rocky hills.

1. What is the main idea of this paragraph?

   _____

   _____

   _____

2. List some of the important details of the paragraph.

   _____

   _____

   _____

   _____

Products. What products might we get from the <u>seven</u> <u>major</u> <u>regions</u> of our country? See if you can put the correct region next to the correct products.

- **Great Lakes** - **Mountain** - **Southwest** - **Northeast**
- **Plains** - **Pacific** - **Southeast**

_____ 1. The main crops are sugarcane, oranges, soybeans, rice, peanuts, and tobacco. The main minerals are oil, iron ore, limestone, and coal. Hickory, oak, maple, and lots of other trees are used for furniture, paper, and other products.

_____ 2. Lots of different kinds of fish and shellfish are found here: cod, butterfish, clams, lobsters, squid, sea bass, flounder, sole, and swordfish. Farm products include milk, cheese, eggs, fruits, vegetables, chickens, turkeys, tomatoes, blueberries, cranberries, maple syrup, and grapes. This region also produces lots of coal.

_____ 3. Record amounts of corn, soybeans, and oats are found here. Other crops include fruits and vegetables. This area is rich in minerals, iron ore, and coal. This area is also rich in dairy products. This is called the "Corn Belt" of the United States.

_____ 4. Corn and wheat grow well here. A lot of farming, ranching, and mining is done here. This area manufactures a lot of hot dogs, flour, and breakfast cereals.

_____ 5. The largest crop in this area is cotton. Other crops are oranges, grapefruit, rice, and wheat. They raise <u>a</u> <u>lot</u> of cattle and sheep here. Silver and copper are found in this region. Fuels are also plentiful, such as coal, natural gas, uranium, and oil.

_____ 6. A wide variety of products come from here because of the two very different climate areas. Products include oil, king crab, salmon, and timber, as well as pineapple, macadamia nuts, fruits, nuts, berries, and vegetables. This area also produces petroleum and natural gas. It has the <u>top</u> agricultural state in the nation, as well as the top commercial fishing region.

_____ 7. Some of the major minerals found in this region are gold, lead, silver, copper, and zinc. There is also lots of natural gas, coal, and oil to be found. Wheat, peas, beans, sugar beets, and potatoes are grown here. Ranching includes beef cattle, sheep, and dairy cows.

Estimating Sums and Differences. When estimating numbers, round them off, then add or subtract. **Remember**: Answers are not exact.

Day 4

EXAMPLE: **420 + 384 = __. 420 is close to <u>400</u>, and 384 is close to <u>400</u>, so your answer would be <u>800</u> when estimating.** Try estimating these problems!

1. 88 + 19 = _____

2. 81 + 75 = _____

3. 93 − 85 = _____

4. 98 − 12 = _____

5. 93 − 39 = _____

6. 891 − 551 = _____

7. 57 − 39 = _____

8. 24 + 35 = _____

9. 209 + 179 = _____

10. 64 + 39 = _____

11. 56 − 33 = _____

12. 288 + 398 = _____

13. 78 − 18 = _____

14. 75 − 42 = _____

15. 540 + 317 = _____

16. 66 + 12 = _____

17. 30 + 71 = _____

18. 610 − 273 = _____

19. 63 + 93 = _____

20. 91 + 65 = _____

21. 247 − 210 = _____

Write the five steps to the writing or composition process. (See page 59 if you need help.) Then write a short story of your own. Use all five steps. You will need additional paper.

Story: _____

_____

_____

_____

_____

_____

_____

_____

_____

_____

_____

_____

_____

Prefixes are syllables added to the beginning of a base word. Add a prefix to these base words. The first one has been done for you.

1. Will you __un__ lock the door?
2. Can you ____call what he said?
3. The brownies seemed to ____appear after the boys saw them.
4. Janet will ____fold the napkins.
5. Do you ____agree with what I said?
6. Mother is going to ____arrange the front room.
7. The picture was the shape of a ____angle.
8. Everyone needs to come ____board now.
9. Erin and Eli will wear ____forms to the game.
10. You can count on me to ____pay you.
11. Look out for the ____coming traffic!
12. The Damons have six ____phones in their house.
13. There is a big ____count on the cost of this table.
14. That was a very ____wise thing to do.

Local, State, and Federal Government Activity. Use a telephone directory to look up listings under local, state, and federal government. Record some at each level.

Telephone Directory

Local	Federal	State
_____	_____	_____
_____	_____	_____
_____	_____	_____
_____	_____	_____
_____	_____	_____
_____	_____	_____
_____	_____	_____

Number Families. You can practice basic math facts by using "families of facts."

$$7 + 2 = 9 \quad 2 + 7 = 9 \quad 9 - 2 = 7 \quad 9 - 7 = 2$$
$$3 \times 6 = 18 \quad 6 \times 3 = 18 \quad 18 \div 3 = 6 \quad 18 \div 6 = 3$$

1 Corinthians 13:6–7
Love...rejoices with the truth. It always protects, always trusts, always hopes, always perseveres.

Day 5

Complete the number families below.

1. 9, 7, 16	**2.** 3, 9, 27

1. 9, 7, 16
$$9 + 7 = 16$$
$$\_\_ + \_\_ = \_\_$$
$$\_\_ - \_\_ = \_\_$$
$$\_\_ - \_\_ = \_\_$$

2. 3, 9, 27
$$3 \times 9 = 27$$
$$\_\_ \times \_\_ = \_\_$$
$$\_\_ \div \_\_ = \_\_$$
$$\_\_ \div \_\_ = \_\_$$

3. 4, 8, 32
$$4 \times 8 = 32$$
$$\_\_ \times \_\_ = \_\_$$
$$\_\_ \div \_\_ = \_\_$$
$$\_\_ \div \_\_ = \_\_$$

4. 8, 5, 40
$$8 \times 5 = 40$$
$$\_\_ \times \_\_ = \_\_$$
$$\_\_ \div \_\_ = \_\_$$
$$\_\_ \div \_\_ = \_\_$$

5. 3, 8, 11
$$3 + 8 = 11$$
$$\_\_ + \_\_ = \_\_$$
$$\_\_ - \_\_ = \_\_$$
$$\_\_ - \_\_ = \_\_$$

6. 3, 4, 12
$$3 \times 4 = 12$$
$$\_\_ \times \_\_ = \_\_$$
$$\_\_ \div \_\_ = \_\_$$
$$\_\_ \div \_\_ = \_\_$$

7. 12, 11, 23
$$12 + 11 = 23$$
$$\_\_ + \_\_ = \_\_$$
$$\_\_ - \_\_ = \_\_$$
$$\_\_ - \_\_ = \_\_$$

8. 612, 208, 820
$$612 + 208 = 820$$
$$\_\_ + \_\_ = \_\_$$
$$\_\_ - \_\_ = \_\_$$
$$\_\_ - \_\_ = \_\_$$

Nouns are words that name people, places, or things.
Common nouns name any person, place, or thing.
Proper nouns name a particular person, place, or thing.
Draw a circle around the common nouns and underline the proper nouns in the following sentences. The first one has been done for you.

1. There are many (missionaries) in Africa.
2. Christopher Columbus was an explorer.
3. Antarctica is a continent.
4. The ships crossed the Atlantic Ocean.
5. We paddled the canoe down the Red River.
6. Astronauts explore space for the United States.
7. San Francisco is the city by the bay.
8. Julie and Ashley visited their aunt in Boston.
9. Mt. Smart is a small mountain in Idaho.
10. Thursday is Andrew's birthday.
11. What state does Mike live in?
12. Are Hilary and her brother going to the circus?
13. Brian went to the library to get some books.

Draw lines between these words and their abbreviations.

EXAMPLE:

Sunday	mag.	dozen	Fri.
magazine	pd.	Friday	tel.
quart	ex.	principal	univ.
November	Sun.	telephone	pt.
paid	oz.	volume	ave.
pages	ft.	pint	Oct.
ounce	Nov.	William	wk.
package	qt.	October	prin.
Doctor	pp.	street	st.
example	govt.	university	Wm.
government	Dr.	week	vol.
foot	pkg.	avenue	doz.

● ●

Our Government. There are three kinds of government: local, state, and federal (or national). Each kind handles problems of different sizes. They try to solve problems that people cannot solve alone. Put the following statements on problem solving and choices in the correct sequence (1, 2, 3, 4).

_____ Write down the possible results of each choice, whether good or bad.

_____ List all the choices or possibilities there are in connection to the problem or situation.

_____ If there is more than one person involved, or if it involves <u>money</u>, people take a vote.

_____ Decide what is most important and which choice or choices will best solve the problem.

Now choose a problem or choice that you are facing and try to follow some or all of the steps above. This problem or choice may affect just you, or it might affect those around you.

Money Sense.

Day 6

1. Cammie has 3 coins worth 11¢. What are the coins?

_____

_____

2. Janet has 6 coins worth 47¢. What are the coins?

_____

_____

3. Frankie has 5 coins worth 17¢. What 5 coins add up to 17¢?

_____

_____

4. Tenley has 7 coins worth 20¢. Find 7 coins with the value of 20¢.

_____

_____

5. Jake has 4 coins. One of them is a quarter. The value of his coins is 45¢. What coins does he have?

_____

_____

6. Gary has 6 coins worth 40¢. Find 6 coins with the value of 40¢.

_____

_____

Singular (One) and Plural (More Than One) Nouns. Write the singular or plural form of the following nouns.

EXAMPLE:

bee _bees_

boys _boy_

1. bunny _____
2. cities _____
3. toe _____
4. buses _____
5. branch _____
6. foot _____
7. sheep _____
8. men _____
9. prayer _____
10. berries _____
11. donkey _____
12. stitch _____
13. oxen _____

14. disciples _____
15. child _____
16. libraries _____
17. movie _____
18. goose _____
19. deer _____
20. boxes _____
21. class _____
22. woman _____
23. tax _____
24. circuses _____
25. turkeys _____
26. book _____

Which word referent should be used in place of the word or words in parentheses? Write it in the blank. <u>He</u>, <u>she</u>, <u>you</u>, <u>it</u>, <u>they</u>, <u>him</u>, <u>her</u>, <u>them</u>, <u>then</u>, <u>here</u>, <u>us</u>, and <u>there</u> are all word referents.

Barbara and Denise were best friends. (Barbara and Denise) _____ had decided to go on a trip together this summer. With maps and brochures scattered all over Barbara's floor, (Barbara and Denise) _____ started looking for a place to go. One brochure described an interesting place. (The brochure) _____ was about Yellowstone Park. "Let's go (Yellowstone) _____!" cried Denise. "(Yellowstone) _____ would be a fun place to go. I think we should ask my brother to go with us," said Barbara. "(My brother) _____ could do a lot of the driving for (Barbara and Denise) _____."

Tom's car was packed and ready to go the next morning. (The car) _____ was a new 4x4 Ranger. (Barbara, Denise, and Tom) _____ would have taken Barbara's car, but (Barbara's) _____ car had a flat tire.

After driving for two days, the travelers got to Yellowstone Park. Tom shouted, "At last we are (at Yellowstone) _____!" (Tom) _____ was tired of driving. (The trip) _____ turned out to be a fun trip for (Denise, Barbara, and Tom) _____.

● ●

Points of Interest. What makes the state, town, or country that you live in an interesting place? Write an advertisement to get people to visit or even live in your state, town, or country. What are the points of interest? What makes it special and different from other places?

_____

_____

_____

_____

_____

_____

_____

Write the number that is <u>10 more</u> than the number shown below, and then write the number that is <u>10 less</u> than the number. The first one is done for you.

Day 7

1. 59	**2.** 496	**3.** 951	**4.** 392
<u>69</u> , <u>49</u>	_____ , _____	_____ , _____	_____ , _____
5. 164	**6.** 703	**7.** 73	**8.** 1,946
_____ , _____	_____ , _____	_____ , _____	_____ , _____

Do the same thing as above, except use <u>100 more</u> than the number and <u>100 less</u> than the number.

9. 150	**11.** 555	**13.** 871	**15.** 3,102
_____ , _____	_____ , _____	_____ , _____	_____ , _____
10. 703	**12.** 493	**14.** 1,956	**16.** 5,691
_____ , _____	_____ , _____	_____ , _____	_____ , _____

Write a proper noun for each of the common nouns listed below.
<u>Remember</u>: Proper nouns start with capital letters.

EXAMPLE:

building *White House*

1. national park _____
2. holiday _____
3. dam _____
4. state _____
5. river _____

6. person _____
7. desert _____
8. day _____
9. island _____
10. street _____

Now write a common noun for the following proper nouns.

1. Golden Gate _____
2. San Francisco _____
3. Pacific _____
4. November _____
5. Canada _____

6. Joseph _____
7. Liberty Bell _____
8. <u>Shut</u> <u>Down!</u> _____
9. Jupiter _____
10. Indians _____

Father's Day. Write about fathers, then draw a picture. Fathers should always... Father should never... If I were a father, I would want to always...

_____

_____

_____

_____

_____

_____

_____

_____

_____

_____

_____

_____   **Draw your picture here!**

_____

_____

_____

_____

_____

_____

_____

_____

_____

_____

Adding Thousands. If you have a  calculator, use it to check your answers.

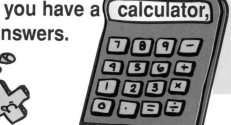

Day 8

| 1. | 2,456
 + 1,527 | 2. | 9,873
 + 1,828 | 3. | 7,125
 + 2,008 | 4. | 4,678
 + 3,321 |

| 5. | 18,086
 + 12,302 | 6. | 8,377
 + 13,674 | 7. | 10,308
 + 23,548 | 8. | 19,873
 + 1,828 |

| 9. | 626
 8,024
 + 3,643 | 10. | 3,481
 309
 + 4,877 | 11. | 1,465
 388
 + 3,035 | 12. | 430
 2,824
 + 4,099 |

A singular (one) possessive noun is usually formed by adding 's—animal's. A plural (two or more) possessive noun is usually formed by adding s'—animals'. Choose a singular or plural possessive noun from the Word Box to fill in the blanks. <u>Hint:</u> Look at the word after the blank to help you decide if you need a singular or plural.

Word Box

birds'
woman's
child's
dog's
children's
Rabbits'
cows'
lady's
plumbers'
Ann's

1. The _____ toy is broken.
2. _____ tails are fluffy.
3. My _____ leash is black.
4. After the accident the _____ tools were all over the road.
5. The _____ pets are in a pet show.
6. The _____ coat is made of fur.
7. We hope that _____ picture will win the prize.
8. The _____ mooing was loud and noisy.
9. That _____ hat blew away in the windstorm.
10. The _____ nests were high up in the trees.

Write the contractions to fill in the circles of the puzzle.

1. I would
2. is not
3. they will
4. should have
5. who are
6. these will
7. must not
8. there have
9. need not
10. it had
11. will not
12. what has
13. might have
14. one is

● ●

Regions of Our Country. Our country is divided into seven regions. <u>Great Lakes</u>, <u>Plains</u>, <u>Mountain</u>, and <u>Pacific</u> are all regions named after bodies of water or important landforms. The other three major regions, <u>Southwest</u>, <u>Southeast</u>, and <u>Northeast</u>, are named for intermediate directions. Label the seven major regions of our United States.

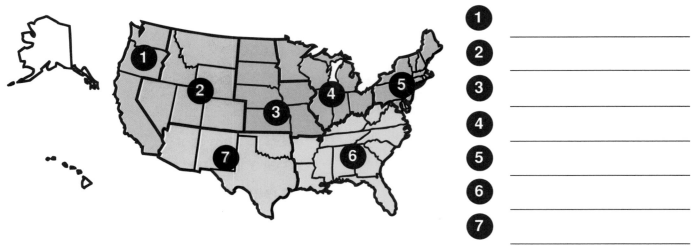

1 _____
2 _____
3 _____
4 _____
5 _____
6 _____
7 _____

*Something to think about. What about Hawaii and Alaska? What region or direction would they belong to?

Hawaii _____ Alaska _____

Subtracting Thousands. Check your answers with a calculator if you have one.

Day 9

1. 8,425
   − 3,519

2. 4,888
   − 1,777

3. 4,314
   − 2,532

4. 3,826
   −   49

5. 9,453
   − 3,168

6. 5,835
   − 1,290

7. 2,182
   − 396

8. 6,922
   − 5,833

9. 8,000
   − 5,603

10. 2,493
   − 1,617

11. 22,318
   − 17,725

12. 57,260
   − 23,458

• •

Write the singular and plural possessive forms of the following nouns. The first one is done for you.

Singular	Possessive	Plural	Possessive
boy	*boy's*	boys	*boys'*
key		keys	
bird		birds	
mouse		mice	
puppy		puppies	
woman		women	
class		classes	
rollerblade		rollerblades	
flag		flags	
computer		computers	

19

Cross out the word that does not belong in the sentence.

EXAMPLE: It's great that we u~~s~~ often agree on things.

1. All butterflies will be gone went by October.
2. Idaho are is known as the "Potato State."
3. She will hid hide behind that large old tree.
4. I have ridden rode my horse regularly this summer.
5. Our dog consistently goes to that corner to dig digging.
6. My baby sister always drinks dranks her milk.
7. Lee Ann had to swept sweep out the garage.
8. I were was very irritated with my friend.
9. How long have you gone go to your church?
10. We have has been forbidden to go into the cave.
11. Have you done did your chores?
12. The scared boy ran run all the way home.
13. He has done did well in all sports.
14. The wind has blew blown for five days.

Time Zones. Unscramble the answers.

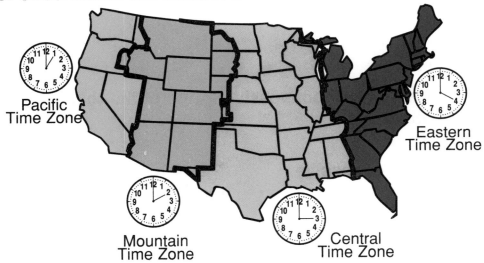

1. Time zones are different because of the <u>usn</u>. _____
2. As we go east the time is <u>treal</u>. _____
3. As we go west the time is <u>rrilaee</u>. _____
4. You can find time zone maps in a <u>lwdro</u> <u>manaacl</u>. _____
5. If you want to find the time in a certain zone to the east you might want to <u>dad</u> <u>suohr</u> _____, not <u>trtbuacs</u> <u>suohr</u>. _____
6. Remember, different parts of the world receive sunlight at different times. That is why we have different <u>meit</u> <u>sonze</u>. _____

Multiplication. Find each product.

EXAMPLE:

1. 9 x 2 = 18

2. 8 x 4 = _____

3. 5 x 6 = _____

4. 7 x 3 = _____

5. 4 x 6 = _____

6. 9 x 5 = _____

7. 8 x 6 = _____

8. 5 x 7 = _____

9. 3 x 9 = _____

10. 7 x 6 = _____

11. 1 x 9 = _____

12. 4 x 7 = _____

13. 8 x 3 = _____

14. 3 x 3 = _____

15. 6 x 3 = _____

16. 6 x 9 = _____

17. 6 x 6 = _____

18. 9 x 4 = _____

19. 7 x 7 = _____

20. 7 x 8 = _____

21. 7 x 9 = _____

22. 9 x 9 = _____

Psalm 71:5
For you have been my hope, O Sovereign LORD, my confidence since my youth.

Day 10

23. 8 x 5 = _____

24. 3 x 4 = _____

25. 5 x 5 = _____

26. 8 x 7 = _____

27. 7 x 3 = _____

28. 8 x 8 = _____

29. 9 x 11 = _____

30. 9 x 10 = _____

31. 9 x 7 = _____

32. 8 x 9 = _____

Main Verbs and Helping Verbs. Helping verbs help the main verb. The main verb shows action. Underline the main verbs. Circle the helping verbs.

EXAMPLE:

1. It (has been) raining for five days.

2. Jack had finished his lessons before 10:00.

3. I have enjoyed the children this month.

4. We were cleaning the house for our friend.

5. The babies have been sleeping for two hours.

6. Two rafts were floating down the river.

Fill in the blank with a helping verb.

7. David _____ diving into the pond.

8. The pool _____ _____ used all summer.

9. I _____ _____ waiting for them to fix it.

10. They _____ _____ working on it for three weeks.

11. It _____ _____ fun without the pool.

12. Seven sheep _____ running loose in the street.

  21

The months of the year and the days of the week are written below in order. On the lines below write the months and days in alphabetical order. Write in cursive.

**January February March April May June July August September
October November December Sunday Monday Tuesday
Wednesday Thursday Friday Saturday**

1. _____
2. _____
3. _____
4. _____
5. _____
6. _____
7. _____
8. _____
9. _____
10. _____
11. _____
12. _____
13. _____
14. _____
15. _____
16. _____
17. _____
18. _____
19. _____

World Globe. Read the information given, then label the following.

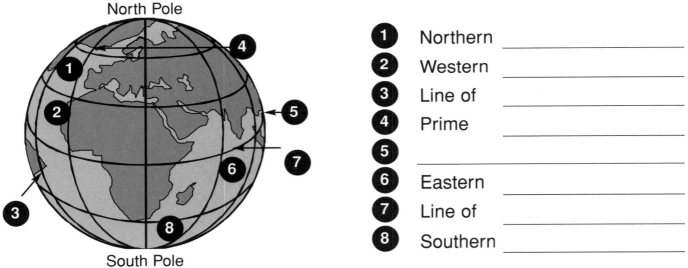

North Pole

South Pole

1 Northern _____
2 Western _____
3 Line of _____
4 Prime _____
5 _____
6 Eastern _____
7 Line of _____
8 Southern _____

We use different terms to locate places on maps and globes. We use lines of latitude to go around the globe from east to west. These lines run parallel to each other, never touching each other. Lines of longitude run north and south on a map or globe and are sometimes called meridians.

The equator is a line of latitude running west to east that divides the earth in half. The top half is called the Northern Hemisphere; the bottom half is called the Southern Hemisphere. The Prime Meridian is a line of longitude. It runs from north to south. All longitudes are determined based on the prime meridian.

Adding or Subtracting Thousands.
Check your answers using a
calculator if you have one.

1. 7,458 − 3,762	2. 8,562 + 2,163	3. 5,585 − 2,609	4. 6,052 − 5,381	5. 7,871 + 1,695
6. 36,814 − 7,523	7. 53,397 + 39,288	8. 19,506 + 34,947	9. 18,103 − 9,079	10. 43,470 − 3,746
11. 3,245 5,029 + 6,981	12. 9,421 8,389 + 4,506	13. 3,340 7,189 + 4,482	14. 46,306 18,782 + 3,115	15. 36,814 17,288 + 29,397

Present tense verbs happen now. Past tense verbs have already happened.
Write the past or present tense for these verbs.

EXAMPLE: **stay—present tense; stayed—past tense.**

Present	Past		Present	Past
1. hop	_____		6. _____	thanked
2. skate	_____		7. _____	called
3. love	_____		8. _____	sprained
4. play	_____		9. _____	wrapped
5. work	_____		10. _____	hugged

Past Tense with a Helper. Write the past tense.

Present Tense	Past Tense with Helping Verb	
EXAMPLE:		
1. walk	has, have, had	*walked*
2. jog	has, have, had	_____
3. pray	has, have, had	_____
4. empty	has, have, had	_____
5. chase	has, have, had	_____

THE PAST TENSE
Time Machine

The Continental Congress adopted the first official American flag in Philadelphia, Pennsylvania, on June 14, 1777. History tells us that at that particular time the thirteen colonies were fighting for their liberty. The flag was a symbol of unity.

Choose one or more of the following activities.

1. Compare our flag today with the first American flag. Write a short paragraph about it.
2. Write what your life may have been like during that time, compared to what it is now.
3. Find out what the stars, stripes, and colors of the flag stand for and write a paragraph.

_____
_____
_____
_____
_____
_____
_____
_____
_____
_____
_____

Your Choice of Rooms. Choose a room in your house and measure the floor space. Measure it in either feet or meters. Draw and label it.

Division. Find each quotient.

Martin Luther King, Jr.: If you lose hope, ...[you lose] that quality that helps you go on in spite of it all. And so today I still have a dream.

Day 12

1. 20 ÷ 4 = _____
2. 28 ÷ 4 = _____
3. 14 ÷ 7 = _____
4. 0 ÷ 2 = _____
5. 42 ÷ 6 = _____
6. 30 ÷ 5 = _____
7. 32 ÷ 4 = _____
8. 25 ÷ 5 = _____
9. 81 ÷ 9 = _____
10. 49 ÷ 7 = _____
11. 18 ÷ 6 = _____
12. 63 ÷ 7 = _____
13. 40 ÷ 5 = _____
14. 36 ÷ 9 = _____
15. 72 ÷ 9 = _____
16. 54 ÷ 6 = _____
17. 48 ÷ 6 = _____
18. 32 ÷ 8 = _____
19. 45 ÷ 9 = _____
20. 36 ÷ 6 = _____
21. 54 ÷ 9 = _____
22. 48 ÷ 8 = _____
23. 63 ÷ 9 = _____
24. 99 ÷ 9 = _____

Fill in the blanks with the past tense verb. <u>Hint:</u> You will have to change the spelling. The first one is done for you.

Past Tense

1. Bells <u>ring</u>. Bells ___*rang*___.
2. We <u>eat</u>. We _____.
3. I <u>wear</u> it. I _____ it.
4. You <u>make</u> some. You _____ some.
5. They <u>sing</u>. They _____.
6. I <u>throw</u>. I _____.
7. I <u>say</u>. I _____.
8. They <u>take</u>. They _____.

Fill in the blank with the past tense of the verb.

9. Sam _____ he wanted to stay in touch with Kit. (know)
10. Katie _____ a letter to Ron. (write)
11. He _____ his friend with him. (bring)
12. The pastor _____ the sermon. (begin)
13. That little girl _____ her doll again. (break)
14. I _____ her new car to the play. (drive)

Replace the word <u>said</u> in these sentences with another word that fits the meaning.

EXAMPLE:

1. The man (said) _____*yelled*_____, "Get that cat out of here!"

2. Margaret (said) _____, "Please, don't do that."

3. Mother always (said) _____, "A stitch in time saves nine."

4. "This is my country," (said) _____ the man with a tall hat.

5. "Is it time to go home so soon?" (said) _____ Mike.

6. "I don't like vegetables in soups," (said) _____ Dad.

7. "My sore throat still hurts," (said) _____ Nicholas.

8. The weatherman (said) _____ that it will be windy today.

9. The boy with a mouth full of candy (said) _____ he wanted more.

10. I called Megan on the phone, and she (said) _____, "There's no school today."

11. The shopkeeper (said) _____, "Do you want red or orange socks?"

12. Kristine Jones (said) _____ her mother makes the best cookies.

● ●

In Genesis 1, the Bible tells us that God created the sun. What else do you know about the sun? Read and then write some interesting facts about the sun. You may want to write about the things you like to do during hot weather when the sun shines.

_____

_____

_____

_____

_____

_____

_____

_____

_____

Multiplication with Three Factors.
Find the product of the three factors.

Joshua 1:9
Be strong and coura-
geous....The LORD your
God will be with you
wherever you go.

Day
13

EXAMPLE: **6 x 1 x 3 = 6 x 1 = 6 x 3 = 18**

1. 2 x 4 x 2 = ___
2. 3 x 3 x 5 = ___
3. 4 x 2 x 2 = ___
4. 2 x 5 x 1 = ___

5. 4 x 2 x 4 = ___
6. 2 x 3 x 7 = ___
7. 0 x 9 x 9 = ___
8. 3 x 2 x 3 = ___

9. 3 x 3 x 3 = ___
10. 5 x 2 x 2 = ___
11. 4 x 2 x 5 = ___
12. 2 x 3 x 6 = ___

13. 1 x 2 x 3 = ___
14. 3 x 3 x 0 = ___
15. 3 x 5 x 0 = ___
16. 1 x 3 x 5 = ___

17. 2 x 3 x 4 = ___
18. 2 x 2 x 3 = ___
19. 4 x 3 x 2 = ___
20. 8 x 1 x 8 = ___

21. 3 x 3 x 8 = ___
22. 3 x 5 x 1 = ___
23. 6 x 3 x 1 = ___
24. 4 x 1 x 3 = ___

Write four sentences using the word <u>are</u>. Write four sentences using the word <u>our</u>. The first two are done for you.

1. <u>Our</u> house is almost finished.
2. When <u>are</u> you going to live in it?
3. _____
4. _____
5. _____
6. _____
7. _____
8. _____

Now write two sentences using <u>it's</u> and <u>its</u>. Remember: <u>It's</u> is a contraction of <u>it is,</u> and <u>its</u> is a possessive pronoun.

1. _____
2. _____
3. _____
4. _____

27

In the Beginning. We're planning a trip back in time—way back in time to the very beginning, when God made the world. You are invited to go back, too. What does it look like when you get there? How does it feel to be there? What are you most excited about seeing? Think, then write!

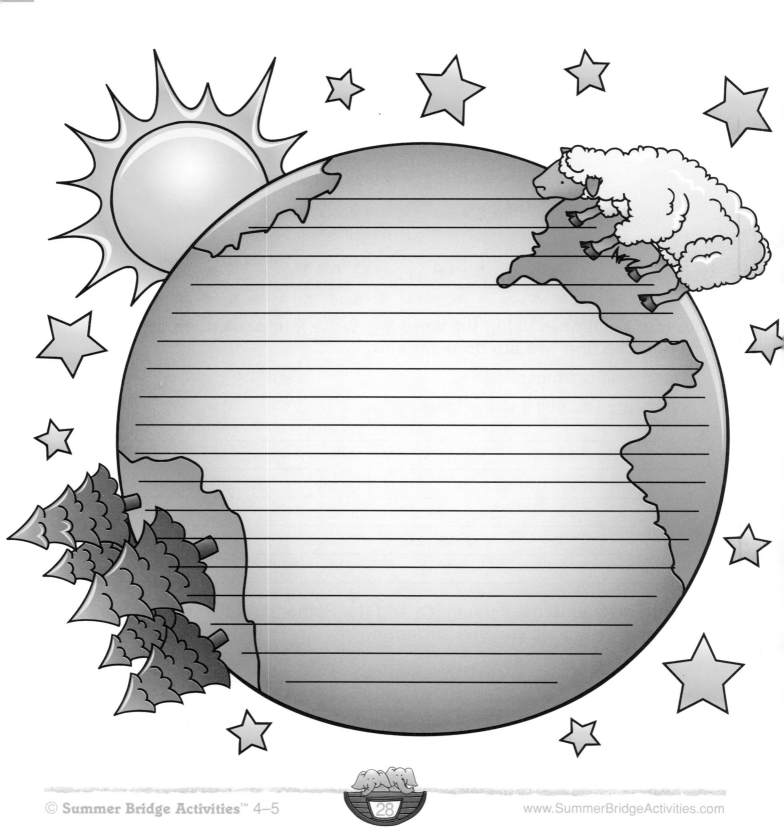

Problem Solving.

Day 14

1. Jennifer bought a package of candy for $2.50. The tax was 19¢. She used a coupon for 42¢ off the price of the candy. How much did she pay?_____

2. Elsie worked at a grocery store keeping the shelves full. She worked 4 hours on Wednesday and 5 hours on Friday. She earned $5 an hour. How much did she earn that week? _____

3. Randy bought a box of cookies for $1.98. He used a 20¢ coupon on "Double Coupon Day." On this particular day, the store took off double the coupon's value. How much did Randy pay for that box of cookies? _____

4. Bradley bought a shirt for $5 off the original price of $24. The tax was $1.40. How much did Bradley pay? _____

5. Gayle bought a 6-pack of canned orange juice for $2.89. The store had a special for 74¢ off the original price. The tax was 60¢. How much did Gayle spend? _____

Match the word to the meaning. Use a dictionary.

EXAMPLE:

1. honorable	a kind of light
2. current	occupation, source of livelihood
3. knowledge	to make clearly known
4. suspicion	good reputation
5. exact	usual, familiar, common
6. lantern	very large, great
7. profession	leaving no room for error
8. universal	now in progress
9. agriculture	uninhabited region
10. declare	all the people born about the same time
11. wilderness	information, awareness, understanding
12. ordinary	humorous, funny
13. comical	understood by all
14. tremendous	the science and art of farming
15. generation	suspecting or being suspected

Here are some words you should know how to spell. Read the meanings below and see if you know what the words mean. Write the word by its meaning.

gnaw   doubt   knit   gnat   glisten   plain
pause   pedal   scene   tow   comfort   admire

1. use long needles to make something out of yarn _____

2. to have high regard for, with wonder and delight _____

3. a lever worked with the foot _____

4. shine or sparkle _____

5. to not believe; to feel unsure _____

6. a short stop or wait _____

7. to pull by a rope or chain _____

8. freedom from hardship; to ease _____

9. flatland; not fancy _____

10. part of a play; show strong feelings in front of others _____

11. to bite at something or wear away _____

12. small fly or insect _____

Continents. Have you ever really looked at the shapes of the continents on a world map? It almost seems as if the continents are part of a big puzzle. Find a world map, then trace and cut out the following major continents and islands: North and South America, Australia, Europe-Asia, Greenland, and Africa. Try to fit all of the continents together so that no (or very little) space exists between them.

Divide to find the quotient.

Acts 27:25
So keep up your courage, men, for I have faith in God that it will happen just as he told me.

1. $4\overline{)28}$　　2. $5\overline{)40}$　　3. $7\overline{)49}$　　4. $6\overline{)30}$

5. $8\overline{)72}$　　6. $9\overline{)45}$　　7. $8\overline{)32}$　　8. $3\overline{)15}$

9. $7\overline{)56}$　　10. $6\overline{)24}$　　11. $7\overline{)14}$　　12. $6\overline{)54}$

13. $9\overline{)9}$　　14. $7\overline{)28}$　　15. $6\overline{)42}$　　16. $8\overline{)56}$

17. $7\overline{)35}$　　18. $6\overline{)48}$　　19. $9\overline{)81}$　　20. $8\overline{)24}$

21. $8\overline{)40}$　　22. $9\overline{)72}$　　23. $7\overline{)63}$　　24. $7\overline{)42}$

Everyone gets scared or nervous about something. Think about what you can do during those times to help you overcome these feelings. Write a story about a time when God gave you courage to fight your fear. Be sure to follow the five steps of the writing process.

_____

_____

_____

_____

_____

_____

_____

_____

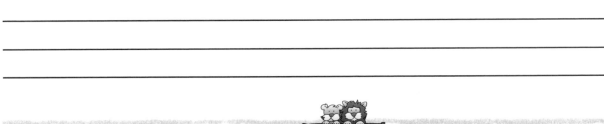

Below are the days of the week and the months of the year spelled with dictionary symbols. Write the words to the side. Don't forget capital letters. The first one is done for you.

1. /ā′prəl/ _____*April*_____

2. /jan′ūre′ē/ _____

3. /mun′dā/ _____

4. /sep tem′bər/ _____

5. /dē sem′bər/ _____

6. /sat′ər dā/ _____

7. /mā/ _____

8. /feb′rüer′ē/ _____

9. /tüz′dā/ _____

10. /frī′dā/ _____

11. /märch/ _____

12. /wenz′dā/ _____

13. /jün/ _____

14. /sun′dā/ _____

15. /nō vem′bər/ _____

16. /o′gest/ _____

17. /thərz′dā/ _____

18. /ok tō bər/ _____

19. /jülī′/ _____

●●●●●●●●●●●●●●●●●●●●●●●●●●●●●●●●●●●●●●

Rocks. Rocks are found almost everywhere. There is much to see and learn about rocks. Geologists are scientists who study rocks. All rocks are made up of one or more minerals. Scientists have discovered over 2,000 minerals. Rocks are changed by water, plants, and other forces of nature.
Below are words you need to know when talking about rocks. Look up each word in the dictionary and write down a short definition for it.

1. igneous _____

2. sedimentary _____

3. metamorphic _____

4. mineral _____

5. crystal _____

6. lava _____

7. magma _____

8. anthracite _____

9. bituminous _____

10. coal _____

Words to Sound, Read, and Spell

ability	comedian	erosion	gravel
accent	commentator	esophagus	graze
acre	convince	essay	gulf
active	cough	estimate	hailstone
adobe	cultural	evaporate	hare
agent	curator	exquisite	harmony
aluminum	custodian	facial	harpsichord
amendment	customs	factor	heirloom
ancestor	dazzling	fake	hemisphere
anchor	deafening	fantasy	herb
appearance	decision	fare	homesteader
appliance	defend	faucet	illustrator
artery	delegate	festival	immigration
assemble	denominator	fever	immune
assuage	deposit	fiction	importance
atmosphere	depth	folklore	income
awkward	desperate	forlorn	incorrect
ballad	diameter	fragile	industry
ballot	diary	freighter	inheritance
barracuda	digit	fret	intersect
bashful	disapprove	frontier	juggler
blunder	disaster	frown	jute
brave	disgraceful	galleon	laboratory
bronze	display	garlic	laryngitis
cafeteria	dormitory	germ	legend
calculator	dose	getaway	lengthen
camouflage	downhearted	ginger	liberty
candidate	drowsy	glamorous	license
canvas	dungeon	gland	lightning
carpenter	earnings	global	limestone
cartoonist	election	grammar	linen
chemical	elegant	grandstand	livestock
clue	engineer	granite	lotion

Words to Sound, Read, and Spell

lounge
luscious
mainland
marble
marionette
mathematics
meadowlark
megaphone
membrane
memoir
messenger
meteor
metric
migration
minerals
misplace
mosquito
musician
muslin
mystery
narrator
nonsense
numerator
nurse
nursery
nylon
obedience
ointment
orchard
organ
outline
oxen
painter

parakeet
parallel
parentheses
password
percale
percussion
perimeter
permission
pharmacist
pianist
population
prescription
press
pretend
professor
pronounce
prop
puppet
quotation
quotient
radius
rattan
recipe
recount
regional
representative
reservoir
revenge
roam
rodent
rotation
rumble
saddle

salve
sameness
scale
schwa
scrapbook
scrawny
sculptor
seaway
section
self-confidence
shipbuilding
shiver
shortage
signature
slender
smear
sodden
soggy
solution
solve
spatula
spice
spine
statehood
statue
stupid
suffer
sunbeam
supermarket
surround
talent
tambourine
tangerine

tarantula
telecast
tender
theft
thrush
title
torrent
tortilla
tract
translator
transplant
transport
treasurer
tributary
tricot
uncertain
uncomfortable
unexpected
unimportant
uninvited
unkind
utensils
verse
vertex
vessel
visible
vitamin
vowel
voyage
wept
wickedness
woodwind
yogurt

Motivational Calendar!

Month _____

My parents and I decided that if I complete 20 days of
Summer Bridge Activities™ *for Young Christians* and
read _____ minutes a day, my incentive/reward will be:

_____

Child's Signature _____ Parent's Signature _____

Day 1 ☆ 🕊 📖 _____		Day 11 ☆ 🕊 📖 _____
Day 2 ☆ 🕊 📖 _____		Day 12 ☆ 🕊 📖 _____
Day 3 ☆ 🕊 📖 _____		Day 13 ☆ 🕊 📖 _____
Day 4 ☆ 🕊 📖 _____		Day 14 ☆ 🕊 📖 _____
Day 5 ☆ 🕊 📖 _____		Day 15 ☆ 🕊 📖 _____
Day 6 ☆ 🕊 📖 _____		Day 16 ☆ 🕊 📖 _____
Day 7 ☆ 🕊 📖 _____		Day 17 ☆ 🕊 📖 _____
Day 8 ☆ 🕊 📖 _____		Day 18 ☆ 🕊 📖 _____
Day 9 ☆ 🕊 📖 _____		Day 19 ☆ 🕊 📖 _____
Day 10 ☆ 🕊 📖 _____		Day 20 ☆ 🕊 📖 _____

Child: Color the ☆ for daily activities completed.
Color the 🕊 for daily devotionals completed.
Color the 📖 for daily reading completed.

Parent: Initial the ____ when all activities are complete.

Jesus loves me!

1. Get a piece of paper that is as long and as wide as you. Lie down on it and have someone outline you with a marker. Then color in the details—eyes, ears, mouth, clothes, arms, hands, etc.

2. Make a "Happy Birthday" card for a friend who is celebrating a birthday and give it to that person on his or her special day.

3. Invite your friends over for popcorn and vote on your favorite movie. Watch the winning movie; then choose parts and act out the movie in your own way.

4. Visit the library and attend story time.

5. With bright colored markers, draw a picture of your favorite place to go. Paste it to a piece of posterboard and cut it into pieces for a jigsaw puzzle.

6. Give your dog a bath or ask your neighbor or friend if you can give their dog a bath.

Fun Activity Ideas to Go Along with the Second Section!

7. Pack a lunch and go to the park.

8. Roast marshmallows over a fire or barbecue.

9. Draw the shape of your state and put a star where you live. Draw your state flower, motto, and bird.

10. Make a batch of cookies and take them to a sick friend, neighbor, or relative.

11. Plant some flower or vegetable seeds in a pot and watch them grow.

12. Organize an earthquake drill for your family.

13. Pick one of your favorite foods and learn how to make it.

14. Write a poem that rhymes.

15. Get your neighborhood friends together and make a card of appreciation for the fire station closest to you. Then all of you deliver the card and take a tour of the station.

16. Prepare a clean bed for your pet.

17. Make and fly a kite.

18. Read to younger children in your family or neighborhood.

19. Invent a new game and play it with your friends.

20. Surprise a family member with breakfast in bed.

www.SummerBridgeActivities.com

Write the rest of the number families.

James Freeman Clarke: Conscience is the root of all true courage; if a man would be brave let him obey his conscience.

Day 1

1. $6 \times 9 = 54$ $9 \times 6 = 54$ $54 \div 6 = 9$ $54 \div 9 = 6$	2. $8 \times 7 = 56$ _____ _____ _____	3. $6 \times 7 = 42$ _____ _____ _____
4. $48 \div 6 = 8$ _____ _____ _____	5. $72 \div 8 = 9$ _____ _____ _____	6. $6 \times 9 = 54$ _____ _____ _____ 7. $32 \div 8 = 4$ _____ _____ _____
8. $36 \div 4 = 9$ _____ _____ _____	9. $9 \times 7 = 63$ _____ _____ _____	10. $5 \times 9 = 45$ _____ _____ _____ 11. $90 \div 9 = 10$ _____ _____ _____

Prefixes and Suffixes. Remember: Prefixes are added to the beginning of a base word. Suffixes are added to the end of a base word. Add a prefix to these words. Use mis-, un-, and re-. Write the whole word.

1. happy _____
2. spell _____
3. build _____

4. judge _____
5. fill _____
6. able _____

Add a suffix to these words. Use -er, -less, -ful, and -ed. Write the whole word.

7. use _____
8. care _____
9. sing _____
10. spell _____

11. hope _____
12. teach _____
13. paint _____
14. report _____

Now write two sentences using words of your choice from each of the two word lists above.

1. _____

2. _____

Opinions. Everyone has an opinion on things that happen around them. People will listen to your opinion more often if you state clearly and plainly why you feel as you do.

Write your opinion on one of the following topics or choose one of your own to write about.

1. People should always wear seatbelts.
2. Children should be able to eat anything they want.
3. Schoolchildren should never have homework to do.
4. We should always help other people, whether they are in our country or not.

_____

_____

_____

_____

_____

_____

_____

_____

_____

_____

_____

_____

_____

_____

_____

_____

_____

_____

_____

_____

I think kids should be able to choose their OWN bedtimes!

Find the product by multiplying.

1 Corinthians 16:13
Be on your guard;
stand firm in the faith;
be men of courage;
be strong.

Day 2

EXAMPLE:
```
  1
 12
x 6
 72
```

1. 12 x 4	**2.** 22 x 6	**3.** 18 x 2

4. 23 x 7	**5.** 34 x 6	**6.** 16 x 5	**7.** 78 x 5	**8.** 93 x 6

9. 86 x 7	**10.** 69 x 9	**11.** 57 x 4	**12.** 62 x 6	**13.** 97 x 7	**14.** 75 x 8

15. 33 x 3	**16.** 21 x 5	**17.** 85 x 8	**18.** 68 x 9	**19.** 45 x 3	**20.** 99 x 9

Think of your five senses to help you describe the words below. Try to come up with a word for each sense.

EXAMPLE:	taste	touch	smell	sight	sound
fire	smoky	hot	smoky	bright	crackle
candy bar	sweet	smooth	chocolate	brown	crunchy

1. a red rose _____

2. a rainbow _____

3. a barnyard_____

4. a snake's skin _____

5. rollerblades _____

6. a snowflake _____

Choose one of the above and write a paragraph about it. Be very descriptive and put in a lot of details.

_____

_____

_____

_____

_____

Prefixes and suffixes can be added to word parts as well as base or root words. Add a prefix or suffix to these word parts, then find and fill in the word shapes below.

1. _du_ plex
2. __ __ mit
3. don __ __
4. sel __ __ __

5. pott __ __ __
6. __ __ __ gress
7. __ __ __ tant
8. syll __ __ __ __

9. __ __ __ dora
10. gran __ __ __
11. __ __ plicate
12. __ __ sent

13. __ __ most
14. fur __ __ __ __
15. __ __ do
16. sta __ __ __ __

[word shape boxes]

_d u p l e x_

Mystery Word. Read the following clues to discover the mystery word.

1. The top layer of the earth's surface.
2. It's composed of mineral particles mixed with animal and plant matter.
3. A well-organized, complicated layer of debris covering most of the earth's land surface.
4. It is shallow in some places and deep in other places.
5. It can be very red or very black, as well as other shades and colors.
6. It is one of the most important natural resources of any country.
7. It is so important that we need to make great efforts to conserve it.
8. It takes a long time for it to form.
9. There are different kinds or types.
10. A geologist thinks of it as material that covers the solid rock below the earth's surface.
11. The engineer thinks of it as material on which to build buildings, roads, earth dams, and landing strips.
12. To the farmer and most other people, it is a thin layer of the earth's surface that supports the growth of all kinds of plants.

The Mystery Word is:

Complete the tables.

Philippians 1:20
I eagerly expect and hope that...Christ will be exalted in my body, whether by life or by death.

Day
3

1. There are 5 pennies in a nickel.

pennies	5	10	15	20	25	30
nickels	1					

2. There are 10 dimes in a dollar.

dimes	10	20	30			
dollars	1	2				

3. There are 6 cans of pop in each carton.

cans	6	12		24		36
cartons	1		3		5	

4. You can get 6 swimming lessons for $20.

lessons	6	12	18			36
money	$20			$80	$100	

When you write something, your reader should be able to understand clearly what you are trying to say. Read the sentences below and change the underlined word to a more descriptive or exact word.

EXAMPLE: This is a <u>good</u> book.
This is an <u>awesome</u> book.

1. My teacher is <u>nice</u>. _____

2. Your <u>things</u> will be safe here. _____

3. That is a <u>big</u> building. _____

4. A car <u>went</u> by our house. _____

5. Our pictures of the trip turned out <u>bad</u>. _____

6. This is a <u>good</u> sandwich. _____

7. The little boy saw a <u>pretty</u> butterfly. _____

8. Goliath was a <u>big</u> man. _____

9. We had a <u>bad</u> winter. _____

10. These grapes are <u>awful</u>. _____

Most words spelled backwards don't mean anything, but some do. Here are clues for some words that become different words when they are written backwards. The first one is done for you.

1. Spell a word backwards for something you cook in, and you will have a word that means siesta. _pan_ & _nap_

2. Spell a word backwards for a name, and you will have something you turn on to get water. _____ & _____

3. Spell a word backwards for something you catch a fish in, and you will have a number. _____ & _____

4. Spell a word backwards for something to carry things in, and you will get a word that tells what you like to do with your friends. _____ & _____

5. Spell a word backwards for something a train needs, and you will get a word for someone who is not honest. _____ & _____

6. Spell a word for "victory" backwards, and you will have a word that means "at once." _____ & _____

7. Spell a word backwards for something to catch a mouse in, and you will get a word that means something less than whole. _____ & _____

8. Spell a word backwards for a tool that cuts wood, and you will get a word that is a verb. _____ & _____

9. Spell a word backwards for a flying mammal, and you will get a word that means "a bill or check." _____ & _____

10. Spell a word backwards for the end of your pen, and you will have a word that means a hole in the ground. _____ & _____

11. Spell a word backwards that means something you bathe in, and you will have a word that means "other than." _____ & _____

12. Spell a word backwards for "an instrument used in doing work," and you will get a word that means "things taken in a robbery." _____ & _____

13. Spell a word backwards for something that means "to have life," and you will get a word that means "wicked." _____ & _____

14. Spell a word backwards for a word that means "a girl," and you will have a word that means "to fall behind." _____ & _____

Measuring in Centimeters. Your little finger is about 1 centimeter wide. If you don't have a centimeter tape, use a string and this centimeter ruler to measure for the following activities.

Day
4

```
+--+--+--+--+--+--+--+--+--+--+--+--+--+--+--+--+
0  1  2  3  4  5  6  7  8  9  10 11 12 13 14 15 16
```

1. The length of your shoes _____
2. The length and width of this book _____, _____
3. Your neck measurement _____
4. Your waist measurement _____
5. Your kitchen table length and width _____, _____
6. The width of a chair in your home _____
7. Your height in centimeters _____
8. The length of the pencil or pen that you use _____

How many other things can you measure? Try estimating, then check to see how close you come to the exact measurement.

_____
_____
_____
_____

● ●

Underline the pronouns in the following sentences. Remember: A pronoun takes the place of a noun.

1. Will you go with us?
2. He did a good job.
3. She went with me.
4. We ate all of them.
5. It is time for her to go.
6. They will help us today.
7. I thanked him for it.
8. You and I need to hurry.
9. Tomorrow we will go to church.
10. This book came for him.
11. A package came for us.
12. You are a good sport.
13. He and I ate the apples.
14. Animals like them also.
15. It was very good.
16. How did she do?

The Fourth of July is our nation's birthday. Another name for it is spelled out in the boxes of the puzzle. Finish the puzzle by writing the appropriate words from the firecrackers. You will not use all of the words.

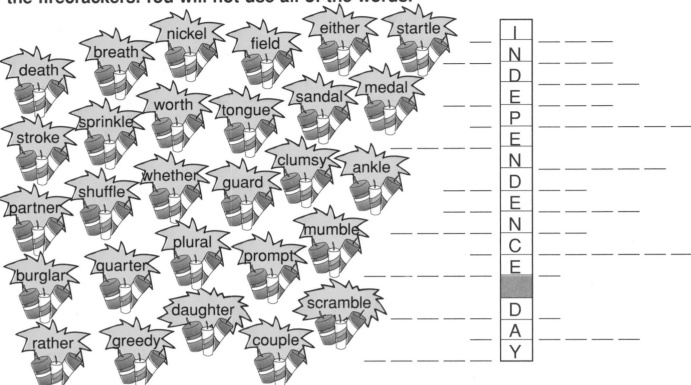

I
N
D
E
P
E
N
D
E
N
C
E

D
A
Y

death, breath, nickel, field, either, startle, medal, worth, sandal, tongue, sprinkle, stroke, clumsy, ankle, whether, shuffle, guard, partner, mumble, plural, quarter, prompt, burglar, daughter, scramble, rather, greedy, couple

Bugs, Bugs, and More Bugs. The world has so many different kinds of bugs, but there's always room for one more. Create a brand new type of bug. Describe it. Where does it live? What does it do? What does it eat? How does it survive? Who are its friends or enemies?

_____

_____

_____

_____

_____

_____

_____

_____

_____

_____

_____

Multiplying with tens and hundreds is fast and fun.

Day 5

1. $4 \times 10 =$ _____

2. $600 \times 6 =$ _____

3. $7 \times 800 =$ _____

4. $30 \times 8 =$ _____

5. $5 \times 20 =$ _____

6. $800 \times 5 =$ _____

7. $8 \times 90 =$ _____

8. $50 \times 6 =$ _____

9. $600 \times 5 =$ _____

10. $4 \times 100 =$ _____

11. $7 \times 80 =$ _____

12. $7 \times 500 =$ _____

13. $900 \times 7 =$ _____

14. $600 \times 4 =$ _____

15. $900 \times 4 =$ _____

16. $8 \times 900 =$ _____

17. $800 \times 2 =$ _____

18. $7 \times 900 =$ _____

19. $3 \times 10 =$ _____

20. $700 \times 6 =$ _____

21. $3 \times 800 =$ _____

22. $7 \times 40 =$ _____

23. $9 \times 10 =$ _____

24. $10 \times 100 =$ _____

25. $4 \times 60 =$ _____

26. $80 \times 2 =$ _____

27. $500 \times 4 =$ _____

28. $7 \times 700 =$ _____

29. $30 \times 8 =$ _____

30. $800 \times 6 =$ _____

31. $9 \times 500 =$ _____

30. $9 \times 300 =$ _____

33. $300 \times 5 =$ _____

Pronouns such as I, you, he, she, it, we, and they can be the subject of a sentence. Read these sentences. The subject is underlined. Rewrite the sentences and use a subject pronoun in place of the underlined subject. Write in cursive.

1. Jim and I went fishing with our dad.

_____

2. The weather was sunny and warm.

_____

3. Ann and Sue can help us with the bait.

_____

4. Mr. Jack broke his leg.

_____

5. Kathy is going to New York on a vacation.

_____

6. Ryan will paint the scenery.

_____

Categorize these words under one of the headings.

Hint: There can be eight words under each heading.

Remember: Categorizing words means to put them in groups that have something in common. One row of examples is given.

interstate	add	region	colony	oxygen	solid
bacteria	city	hemisphere	stop	column	inch
debate	larva	yield	basin	hexagon	canal
environment	speed	equal	fossil	candidate	intersection
measure	insect	bay	caution	map	estimate
numerator	freedom	society	elevation	freeway	railroad
patriot	habitat	civilization	mineral	detour	quotient

Math Words	Geography Words	Transportation Words	Science Words	Social Studies Words
add	*region*	*interstate*	*bacteria*	*colony*

What about These Animals in Our Country? Buffalo, condors, and grizzly bears have all but disappeared from our country. The symbol of our country, the bald eagle, is very rare in most states. Bald eagles and bears live in mountainous regions. Prairie dogs and antelope live on the plains. Alligators live in marshy areas. Rattlesnakes live in the desert. Wild turkeys can be found in wilderness areas. These are all animals found in our country. There are also many others. Choose one of the following to do on a separate piece of paper.

1. Choose and draw a picture of an animal from our country. Place it in the correct habitat. Color it accurately. What other interesting animals do you think might belong in this area? Draw them. What other important information does your picture show?

2. If you choose not to draw a picture about an animal, write a paragraph about one. Use the same type of information that the picture would portray.

What animal(s) did you choose? _____

_____

_____

Addition and multiplication are related. Answer the addition problems and then write the related multiplication problem.

Day
6

EXAMPLE: 10 + 10 + 10 + 10 + 10 = 50 or 5 x 10 = 50

1. 20 + 20 + 20 = _____   _____ x _____ = _____

2. 9 + 9 + 9 + 9 + 9 + 9 = _____   _____ x _____ = _____

3. 100 + 100 + 100 + 100 = _____   _____ x _____ = _____

4. 8 + 8 + 8 + 8 + 8 + 8 + 8 + 8 = _____   _____ x _____ = _____

5. 12 + 12 + 12 + 12 = _____   _____ x _____ = _____

6. 75 + 75 + 75 = _____   _____ x _____ = _____

7. 35 + 35 + 35 + 35 + 35 + 35 = _____   _____ x _____ = _____

8. 51 + 51 + 51 + 51 + 51 = _____   _____ x _____ = _____

Use the pronouns me, her, him, it, us, you, and them after action verbs. Use I and me after the other nouns or pronouns. Circle the correct pronoun in each sentence.

1. Lily and (I, me) like to visit museums.
2. (They, Them) were very juicy oranges.
3. He helped her and (I, me) sing the hymn.
4. (We, Us) tried not to fall as much this time.
5. Miss Green gave a shovel and bucket to (he, him).
6. (I, Me) wanted a new horse for Christmas.
7. Rick asked (she, her) to come with us.
8. Jason went with (they, them) to the mountain.
9. Mother asked (I, me) to fix the dinner.
10. Carla got some forks for (we, us).
11. Please, teach that trick to Lisa and (I, me).
12. She and (I, me) swam all day.

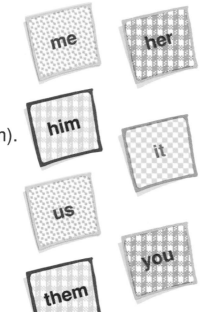

Study this table about trees, and use it to answer the questions below. Can you identify the trees around you?

Tree	Bark	Wood	Leaves
Elm	brown and rough	strong	oval-shaped, saw-toothed edges, sharp points
Birch	creamy white, peels off in layers	elastic, won't break easily	heart-shaped or triangular with pointed tips
Oak	dark gray, thick, rough, deeply furrowed	hard, fine-grained	round, finger-shaped lobes
Willow	rough and broken	brown, soft, light	long, narrow, curved at tips
Maple	rough gray	strong	grow in pairs and are shaped like your open hand
Hickory	loose, peels off	white, hard	shaped like spearheads
Christmas Holly	ash colored	hard and fine-grained	glossy, sharp-pointed

1. Which tree has heart-shaped leaves? _____ Hand-shaped?

   _____

2. How many trees have hard wood? _____

3. Which trees have sharp-pointed leaves? _____

4. Which tree has wood like a rubber band? _____

5. How many different colors of bark does the table show? _____

   Name them _____

6. Which tree do you think we get syrup from? _____

7. Which tree bark do you think Indians used to cover their canoes?

   _____

8. Which wood do you think is best for making furniture? _____,

   _____, and _____

9. Why do you think the holly tree is called Christmas Holly? _____

10. Look around your yard and neighborhood. Can you identify any of the trees

    from the table? If so, which ones? _____

Complete this multiplication table.

x	10	20	30	40	50	60	70	80	90
1	10	20					70		
2						120			
3		60							270
4				160					
5							350		
6									
7			210						
8						480			
9				360					

Day 7

How does multiplying by hundreds differ from multiplying by tens?

_____

Could you change this table to show multiplying by hundreds?

_____

How? _____

Using Its, It's, Your, and You're. It's and you're are contractions. Its and your are possessive pronouns. Fill in the blanks with it's, its, your, or you're.

1. I hope _____ coming to my bonfire.
2. The bonfire will be for _____ friends also.
3. Do you think _____ too warm for a bonfire?
4. _____ starting time is eight o'clock.
5. Will _____ family come to the bonfire with you?
6. _____ base is long and wide.
7. _____ coming early, aren't you?
8. I think I will need _____ help.
9. _____ going to last about four hours.
10. _____ bound to be a lot of fun.

Write a sentence of your own for each word.

11. it's_____
12. its _____
13. you're _____
14. your _____

Read this crazy story. Every time you come to an underlined word, write the abbreviation for it. The first one is done for you.

Last January _Jan._ we moved from Georgia _____ to New York _____. It was a very long trip. We had to walk most of the way because the car broke down. We left on Monday _____, March _____ 10 and didn't get there until five years _____ later.

On the trip, I had to learn how to measure. One day I measured gallons _____, inches, _____, yards _____, and grams _____. I also learned about science _____, adverbs _____, and adjectives _____. It was a boring trip!

We only traveled about two miles per hour _____. That's why it took us so long. Also, we stopped at a number _____ of relatives' places and stayed for months _____ on end.

Next time, let's fly!

● ●

Name an animal or insect that begins with the letters given. If there is not one that begins with that letter, leave it blank or put an X in the box.

	s	d	r	t
insects				
birds				
reptiles				
rodents				
spiders				
zoo animals				
wild animals				
farm animals				
ocean animals				
dinosaurs				

What about Time? You know that 60 seconds = 1 minute, 60 minutes = 1 hour, 24 hours = 1 day, 7 days = 1 week, 52 weeks = 1 year, 12 months = 1 year, and 365 days = 1 year (except leap year, which has 366 days).

Philippians 1:6
...He who began a good work in you will carry it on to completion until the day of Christ Jesus.

Day 8

Use what you know to complete the following.

1. Phillip is in the fourth grade. He is 10 _____ old.
2. There are 30 _____ in June.
3. Nancy's baby brother started to walk at the age of 11 _____.
4. We have 48 _____ in 2 days.
5. Nick's swimming lesson is 25 _____ long.
6. It took Leslie 10 _____ to complete her daily devotions.
7. Mother's Day is celebrated once a _____.
8. Many children get about 3 _____ summer vacation.
9. It takes about 1 _____ to blink your eyes.
10. Most children go to school 5 _____ a week.
11. There are 30 _____ in half a minute.
12. It took Monica 2 and a half _____ to do all her chores.

Write these words in alphabetical order. Be sure to look at the third or fourth letters.

1. events, evening, every, eventually

_____ _____ _____ _____

2. tremendous, treatment, tree, treasure

_____ _____ _____ _____

3. coast, coconut, coal, collect, color

_____ _____ _____ _____ _____

4. entrance, entry, end, enthusiasm, enough

_____ _____ _____ _____ _____

5. grandfather, graph, grain, grateful, grab, graduated

_____ _____ _____ _____ _____ _____

What Does It Really Mean? Write what you think
these idiomatic expressions mean.

1. She was really <u>pulling</u> <u>my</u> <u>leg</u>. _____

2. Do you think we'll <u>be</u> <u>in</u> <u>hot</u> <u>water</u>? _____

3. If you don't <u>button</u> <u>your</u> <u>lip</u>, I'll scream! _____

4. Sonny, please <u>get</u> <u>off</u> <u>my</u> <u>back</u>! _____

5. When you are having fun, <u>time</u> <u>flies</u>. _____

6. You've <u>hit</u> <u>it</u> <u>on</u> <u>the</u> <u>head</u>, Andrew. _____

7. Ryan will <u>lend</u> <u>a</u> <u>hand</u> tomorrow. _____

8. In the winter, my bedroom is <u>like</u> <u>an</u> <u>icebox</u>. _____

9. Mrs. Tune always has beautiful flowers; she <u>must</u> <u>have</u> <u>a</u> <u>green</u> <u>thumb</u>.

_____

10. My brother's stomach is <u>a</u> <u>bottomless</u> <u>pit</u>. _____

A Litter Graph. Go on a "litter" walk. In a plastic bag,
gather up litter as you go. Only pick up <u>safe</u> litter. Do
not pick up anything marked hazardous waste, needles,
or litter you are unsure of. When you are finished, bring
it home. Categorize what you have found and display it
in a bar graph.

Type of Litter	1	2	3	4	5	6	7	8	9	10	more than 10

Place Value Division Patterns. We know that 8 ÷ 2 = 4, so 80 ÷ 2 = 40, and 800 ÷ 2 = 400. Do the following division patterns.

Aristotle: Moral excellence comes about as a result of habit. We become just by doing just acts, temperate by doing temperate acts...

Day 9

1. 9 ÷ 3 = _____   90 ÷ 3 = _____   900 ÷ 3 = _____
2. 8 ÷ 2 = _____   80 ÷ 2 = _____   800 ÷ 2 = _____
3. 12 ÷ 4 = _____   120 ÷ 4 = _____   1,200 ÷ 4 = _____
4. 6 ÷ 3 = _____   60 ÷ 3 = _____   600 ÷ 3 = _____
5. 30 ÷ 6 = _____   300 ÷ 6 = _____   3,000 ÷ 6 = _____
6. 72 ÷ 8 = _____   720 ÷ 8 = _____   7,200 ÷ 8 = _____
7. 32 ÷ 8 = _____   320 ÷ 8 = _____   3,200 ÷ 8 = _____
8. 49 ÷ 7 = _____   490 ÷ 7 = _____   4,900 ÷ 7 = _____
9. 56 ÷ 8 = _____   560 ÷ 8 = _____   5,600 ÷ 8 = _____
10. 25 ÷ 5 = _____   250 ÷ 5 = _____   2,500 ÷ 5 = _____
11. 40 ÷ 8 = _____   400 ÷ 8 = _____   4,000 ÷ 8 = _____
12. 63 ÷ 9 = _____   630 ÷ 9 = _____   6,300 ÷ 9 = _____

Look up the word <u>meet</u> in a dictionary. At the end of each sentence, write what part of speech (noun or verb) <u>meet</u> is. Then write the number for the meaning of the word <u>meet</u>. The first one is done for you.

EXAMPLE: I will <u>meet</u> you at three.   _Verb — 2_

1. Tomorrow we are going to have a track <u>meet</u>.   _____
2. I hope he doesn't <u>meet</u> with disaster.   _____
3. We need to <u>meet</u> the plane at seven P.M.   _____
4. He will have to <u>meet</u> the payments every month.   _____
5. It was nice to <u>meet</u> and talk with you yesterday.   _____
6. Are you going to <u>meet</u> us at youth group tonight?   _____

Someone with Strength. What is strength? Choose someone from the Bible known for having amazing strength. Write about this person. How did the person get strength? How did the person use strength? Could the person lose it?

_____

_____

_____

_____

_____

_____

_____

_____

_____

_____

_____

_____

_____

_____

_____

_____

_____

_____

_____

_____

_____

_____

Find the quotients and the remainders. Use a separate piece of paper to show your work.

Day 10

EXAMPLE:

$$3 \overline{)38} = 12 \textbf{ R } 2$$
$$\underline{3}$$
$$8$$
$$\underline{6}$$
$$2$$

1. $2\overline{)65}$

2. $5\overline{)57}$

3. $3\overline{)95}$

4. $4\overline{)85}$

5. $9\overline{)100}$

6. $3\overline{)37}$

7. $4\overline{)47}$

8. $5\overline{)58}$

9. $7\overline{)79}$

10. $4\overline{)87}$

11. $3\overline{)68}$

12. $4\overline{)35}$

Draw a line between the syllables. First, try to <u>remember</u> what you have learned about where to divide them. Then use a dictionary if you need more help.

EXAMPLE: col/or

1. column
2. inflate
3. slashing
4. pigeon
5. afraid
6. frozen
7. tennis
8. harness
9. gable

10. alphabet
11. soviet
12. bicycle
13. difficult
14. kerosene
15. liveliness
16. glorious
17. understood
18. jewelry

19. generation
20. vegetable
21. evidence
22. memory
23. quality
24. splendid
25. museum
26. hospital
27. ordinary

The next time you watch TV or read a magazine, look at the commercials or ads. In the boxes below, write down what you think is true about the commercials or ads and what you think is false.

What is the commercial or ad about?	TRUE	FALSE
	1.	1.
	2.	2.
	3.	3.
	4.	4.
	5.	5.

Conserving Energy. Recycling saves energy and natural resources. Besides recycling, how can we conserve energy? Write down ways to conserve energy with the following:

water _____

lights _____

heat _____

electricity _____

transportation _____

cold weather _____

refrigerator _____

buying things _____

bathroom _____

Write the fraction that describes the shaded section.

1 John 2:28
Continue in him, so that when he appears we may be confident and unashamed before him at his coming.

Day 11

EXAMPLE:

1. $\dfrac{1}{2}$

2. _____

3. _____

4. _____

5. _____

6. _____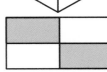

7. _____

8. _____

9. _____

10. _____

11. _____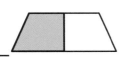

12. _____

A dictionary gives us a lot of information about words. Look up the following words in a dictionary and write down the special spelling of each. Also write down a short definition for each word.

	Word	Special Spelling	Definition
1.	blue•bon•net	**blü´bon´net**	the cornflower
2.	mas•sive		
3.	suit•case		
4.	cir•cus		
5.	glox•in•i•a		
6.	rig•ging		
7.	di•lem•ma		
8.	meas•ure		
9.	stu•dent		
10.	un•or•gan•ized		
11.	def•i•ni•tion		
12.	yaws		
13.	re•spect		
14.	blun•der•buss		

Practice writing and spelling these homonyms. Write in cursive. After you know how to spell them, have someone give you a test to see if you can spell them without looking. Write each word twice.

way	_____	_____	sight	_____	_____
weigh	_____	_____	site	_____	_____
base	_____	_____	arc	_____	_____
bass	_____	_____	ark	_____	_____
threw	_____	_____	tide	_____	_____
through	_____	_____	tied	_____	_____
scene	_____	_____	waist	_____	_____
seen	_____	_____	waste	_____	_____
			sore	_____	_____
			soar	_____	_____
			pare	_____	_____
			pair	_____	_____
			pear	_____	_____

Water in the Air. There is water in the air. How does it get there? Clouds and rain are made from water vapor in the air.

Try this to help explain how water gets into the air. Take 3 or more drinking glasses that are all about the same size. Fill the glasses almost full of water. Place them in different areas such as warm places, cool places, dark places, windy places, outside places, inside places, and other places of your choice. Watch them for 4 or 5 days or longer. Check the water levels. What happened to the water in the glasses? Where did it go? Explain in your own words where you think the water vapor in the atmosphere comes from and where it goes.

_____

_____

_____

_____

_____

_____

Comparing Fractions. Use the fraction table to help find out which fraction is greater and which fraction is less. Use >, <, or =.

Day 12

1. $\frac{1}{2}$ ◯ $\frac{1}{4}$ 2. $\frac{2}{3}$ ◯ $\frac{1}{3}$

3. $\frac{1}{4}$ ◯ $\frac{1}{6}$ 4. $\frac{2}{6}$ ◯ $\frac{1}{3}$

5. $\frac{4}{8}$ ◯ $\frac{2}{10}$ 6. $\frac{1}{12}$ ◯ $\frac{1}{10}$

7. $\frac{3}{4}$ ◯ $\frac{2}{8}$ 8. $\frac{2}{5}$ ◯ $\frac{1}{3}$

9. $\frac{3}{8}$ ◯ $\frac{10}{12}$ 10. $\frac{2}{8}$ ◯ $\frac{1}{4}$

11. $\frac{1}{5}$ ◯ $\frac{2}{10}$ 12. $\frac{1}{3}$ ◯ $\frac{2}{4}$

13. $\frac{1}{6}$ ◯ $\frac{1}{3}$ 14. $\frac{3}{12}$ ◯ $\frac{1}{3}$

15. $\frac{5}{10}$ ◯ $\frac{3}{6}$ 16. $\frac{1}{2}$ ◯ $\frac{6}{10}$

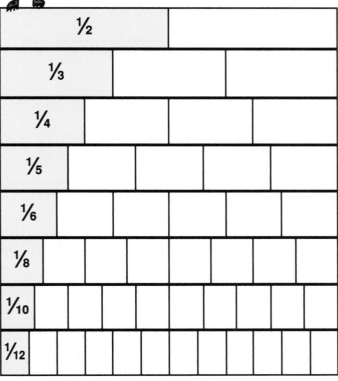

Write a short report. <u>Remember</u>: A report is only facts about a topic. Look in an encyclopedia for help. Follow these steps: Choose a topic and plan your report, write, revise, proofread, and make a final copy.

These letters are in alphabetical order. See if you can make a word from them. The first letter is underlined.

EXAMPLE:

1. abbelopr   **probable**
2. aejlosu _____
3. eeenprrst _____
4. beeemmrr _____
5. beknnoru _____
6. cdffiilut _____
7. accdginor _____
8. eegmnnortv _____
9. aaegimnz _____

10. eiorssu _____
11. ghhottu _____
12. irstw _____
13. aeginrv _____
14. dinrstuy _____
15. ceenrt _____
16. ehilstw _____
17. ainosux _____
18. deilors _____
19. aabeggg _____
20. elrtuuv _____

Put the letters in these words in alphabetical order.

21. heaven _____
22. fountain _____
23. basement _____
24. factory _____

25. hospital _____
26. committee _____
27. paragraph _____
28. kingdom _____

Blow Up a Balloon. Here is an experiment that you can do in your home with an adult's permission. Get a balloon and blow it up several times until the balloon becomes easy to enlarge. Put one tablespoon of baking soda in the balloon, then put 3 tablespoons of white vinegar into a soda pop bottle. Now put the balloon opening around the mouth of the soda pop bottle. Move the balloon so the baking soda falls down and mixes with the vinegar. Draw a picture of what happens and write a couple of sentences to go with your picture.

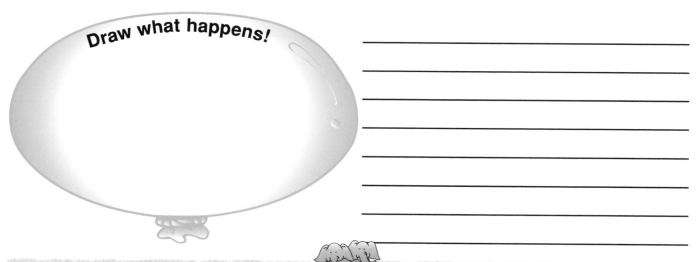

Draw what happens!

_____
_____
_____
_____
_____
_____
_____

Multiplying 3-digit numbers by 1-digit numbers.

EXAMPLE:

6 x 3 = 18   3 x 80 = 240   3 x 100 = 300
               18 + 240 + 300 = 558

21
186
x 3
558

Day 13

1. 162
   x 5

2. 398
   x 2

3. 904
   x 8

4. 329
   x 5

5. 240
   x 7

6. 432
   x 6

7. 412
   x 8

8. 542
   x 9

9. 506
   x 5

10. 554
    x 6

11. 473
    x 9

12. 257
    x 8

Put commas in the following sentences to separate words in a series.

1. Nan Tom Julie and James are going to a movie.
2. Anne took her spelling reading and math books to school.
3. The snack bar is only open on Monday Tuesday Friday and Saturday.
4. The plaid skirt was blue green yellow black and orange.
5. Women men children and pets enjoy sledding.
6. Have you ever seen baby kittens piglets or goslings?
7. Carla and Mark bought postcards film candy and souvenirs.

Now write four sentences of your own. Name at least three people, sports, or foods in a series. Be sure to put in the commas.

8. _____

9. _____

10. _____

11. _____

Your Life. What do you think God has planned for you to do with your life? What kinds of gifts and talents have you been given? How can you use those to live for the Lord? Think and write about it.

_____

_____

_____

_____

_____

_____

_____

_____

_____

_____

_____

_____

_____

_____

_____

_____

_____

_____

_____

_____

_____

_____

_____

How Many Times in a Minute? Use a watch with a minute hand or a stopwatch to time yourself as you do the following activities. Use that information to calculate how many times you could do those things in 5 minutes, 8 minutes, 10 minutes, and 15 minutes.

Day 14

1. How far can you hop in a minute? _____

2. How far can you walk in a minute? _____

3. How many jumping jacks can you do in a minute? _____

4. How many times can you toss a ball and catch it in a minute? _____

5. How many times can you bounce a ball in a minute? _____

6. How many times do you breathe in a minute? _____

7. How many times does your heart beat in a minute? _____

8. How many times can you write your name in a minute? _____

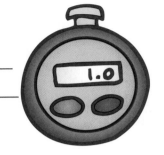

Activity	Minutes				
	1	5	8	10	15
hop					
walk					
jumping jacks					
toss and catch ball					
bounce ball					
breathe					
heart beats					
write name					

Put commas after <u>yes</u> or <u>no</u> when they begin a sentence and before and/or after names when that person is being spoken to. Put the commas in these sentences.

1. Yes I will go with you John.

2. Kirk do you want to go?

3. No I need to finish this.

4. John I am glad Sam will come.

5. Nicky what happened?

6. Don I fell on the sidewalk.

7. Aaron do you play tennis?

8. No Eli I never learned how.

9. Come on B.J. let's go to the game.

10. Yes I was x-rayed at the doctor's.

11. Mom thanks for the help.

12. Tell me Joe did you do this?

13. Yes but I'm sorry I did.

14. Well Joe try to be more careful next time.

15. Okay Dad I'll never do it again.

16. George do you like basketball?

Do you know when the holidays come? Fill in the blanks with the date or name of the correct holiday. Use a calendar if you need help.

1. In December, we celebrate Jesus' birth on _____

2. On January 1, we celebrate _____ _____ _____ .

3. In May, we have _____ _____ .

4. Be sure to wear green in March. It's _____ _____ _____ .

5. In October 1492, he sailed the ocean blue. _____ _____ .

6. On February 14, be sure to send your sweetheart a _____ .

7. On July 4, we celebrate _____ _____ .

8. Sometimes it comes in March; sometimes it comes in April: _____ .

9. Do you work on _____ _____ in September?

10. _____ and _____ also have birthdays in February.

11. In June, we also have _____ _____ .

12. Martin Luther King Jr.'s birthday is in _____ .

13. Because the Pilgrims came, we have _____ .

14. _____ _____ is in June.

15. On November 11, we honor our _____ .

Word Search. Find and circle words that harm our environment.

c	a	r	s	i		p	o	c	a	l	o	c	t	w
j		l	o	p	p	o	s	f		i	d	h	s	r
f	a	c	t	o	r	i	e	s	g	t	a	d	n	a
p	k	n	s	l	a	s	w	a	s	t	e		s	p
l	c	g		l	g	o	a	e	b	e	i	e	h	p
r	a	q	s	u	u	n	g	d	w	r	l	m	l	e
b	r	n	b	t	m	k	e	s	i	t	t	e	a	r
b	a	t	j	i	l	l	k	m	t	b	k	m	n	s
c	a	r	b	o	n		m	o	n	o	x	i	d	e
v	u	a	f	n	j	c	b	g	m	e		s	f	a
p	t	s	f	l	o	o	d	s	i	d	l	g	i	z
s	o	h	s	t	r	i	n	g	r	a	g	s	l	r
t		s	p	e	o	p	l	e	c	s	t	y	l	t
u	e	t	r	p	e	s	t	i	c	i	d	e	s	s
g	x	v	e	c	k		m	a	n	c	f	o	e	n
n	h	x	o	n	a	e	h	g	l	a	s	s	e	o
o	a	c	u	b	h	g	a	r	b	a	g	e	u	t
w	u	j	a	c	f	a	c	t		p	a	p	e	r
	s	t	y	r	o	f	o	a	m	v	a	r	m	a
s	t	u	f	f		g	n	p	l	a	s	t	i	c

litter
bottles
garbage
trash
cars
people
rags
smoke
waste
pollution
cans
landfills
stuff
junk
auto exhaust
carbon monoxide
factories

gum
cartons
poison
chemicals
paper
styrofoam
pesticides
sewage
bags
smog
weeds
floods
wrappers
plastic
string
glass

Find the quotient and the remainder by division.

2 Chronicles 20:20 "...Have faith in the LORD your God and you will be upheld..."

Day 15

1. 8)963

2. 2)741

3. 8)960

4. 4)561

5. 7)915

6. 8)887

7. 5)753

8. 4)882

9. 9)918

10. 7)716

11. 3)919

12. 9)908

13. 4)835

14. 9)967

15. 8)842

16. 3)667

17. 5)182

18. 6)424

19. 4)392

20. 6)438

21. 7)948

22. 6)787

23. 4)721

24. 8)736

Using Punctuation Marks. Put periods and question, exclamation, and quotation marks in the following sentences. Use proper capitalization.

1. Nate, do you have the map of our town asked Kit
2. What an exciting day I had cried Mary
3. I said the puppy fell into the well
4. Did you learn that birds' bones are hollow asked Mrs. Tippy
5. She answered No, I did not learn that
6. Wayne exclaimed I won first prize for the pie eating contest
7. I'm tired of all work and no play said Sadie
8. I agree with you replied Sarah
9. Mr. Harris said this assignment is due tomorrow
10. It will be part of your final grade he added

Circle the two words in each group that are spelled correctly.

A	**B**	**C**	**D**	**E**
gabel	suger	allready	where	jackit
genuine	surpize	among	weather	junior
gracefull	terrible	aunte	wite	jujment
graine	straight	awhile	weare	justece
great	sonday	addvise	rotee	journey

F	**G**	**H**	**I**	**J**
rimind	feathers	donkiys	handsum	explore
remain	feever	doubble	herrd	elctrecity
fouff	finsih	drawer	holiday	enjine
refer	folow	dosen	healthy	enormous
raisd	fiction	detective	haevy	ecstat

Complete the picture and add what other details you would like.

Equal Fractions.
Use the fraction table on page 59 to find equal fractions. You could make your own fraction table!

Day 16

1. $\dfrac{1}{3} = \dfrac{}{6}$

2. $\dfrac{4}{5} = \dfrac{}{10}$

3. $\dfrac{10}{10} = \dfrac{}{6}$

4. $\dfrac{}{5} = \dfrac{4}{10}$

5. $\dfrac{4}{16} = \dfrac{}{8}$

6. $\dfrac{12}{12} = \dfrac{}{10}$

7. $\dfrac{3}{6} = \dfrac{}{12}$

8. $\dfrac{9}{12} = \dfrac{}{4}$

9. $\dfrac{}{9} = \dfrac{4}{6}$

10. $\dfrac{0}{4} = \dfrac{}{2}$

11. $\dfrac{6}{8} = \dfrac{}{4}$

12. $\dfrac{1}{2} = \dfrac{}{10}$

13. $\dfrac{}{4} = \dfrac{4}{8}$

14. $\dfrac{3}{9} = \dfrac{}{3}$

15. $\dfrac{}{15} = \dfrac{2}{3}$

16. $\dfrac{2}{3} = \dfrac{}{12}$

17. $\dfrac{}{3} = \dfrac{6}{18}$

18. $\dfrac{}{15} = \dfrac{3}{5}$

19. $\dfrac{}{6} = \dfrac{2}{3}$

20. $\dfrac{}{8} = \dfrac{1}{4}$

21. $\dfrac{3}{6} = \dfrac{}{2}$

22. $\dfrac{1}{3} = \dfrac{}{9}$

23. $\dfrac{6}{9} = \dfrac{}{3}$

24. $\dfrac{}{6} = \dfrac{3}{18}$

What Does It Mean? Choose a word from the word bank and write it next to the correct meaning.

Word Bank

schedule
assistant
campaign
approximately
hollow
exchange
university
venture
artificial
publicity
harness
estate
reputation
genuine

1. not natural, not real _____

2. a timed plan for a project _____

3. a giving or taking of one thing for another _____

4. esteem in which a person is commonly held _____

5. a person who serves or helps _____

6. really being what it is said to be; true or real _____

7. a series of organized, planned actions _____

8. to make information commonly known _____

9. near in position _____

10. an educational institution of the highest level _____

11. having a cavity within it, not solid _____

12. something on which a risk is taken _____

13. one's property or possessions _____

14. connects an animal to a plow or vehicle _____

Look at the homonyms you spelled on page 58. Choose five pairs of these and write a sentence for each one.

EXAMPLE: way/weigh

I could not see him; we were <u>way</u> down the road.
How much do you <u>weigh</u>?

1. _____

_____

2. _____

_____

3. _____

_____

4. _____

_____

5. _____

_____

First-Aid Kit. Every home should have a first-aid kit. This enables the family to have many types of bandages and medicines in one place, should they be needed.

Make a list of things you think should be in a first-aid kit. When you are finished, check with your parents to see if you have all the basic things listed for a first-aid kit. If your family has one, ask your parents to go through it with you.

Adding Fractions.

$\frac{2}{3} + \frac{1}{3} = \frac{3}{3}$ ← add the numerator
← use the same denominator

Day 17

1. $\frac{1}{3} + \frac{1}{3} =$

2. $\frac{1}{2} + \frac{1}{2} =$

3. $\frac{6}{12} + \frac{5}{12} =$

4. $\frac{6}{12} + \frac{7}{12} =$

5. $\frac{5}{8} + \frac{2}{8} =$

6. $\frac{3}{10} + \frac{4}{10} =$

7. $\frac{1}{6} + \frac{2}{6} =$

8. $\frac{11}{12} + \frac{11}{12} =$

9. $\frac{7}{10} + \frac{1}{10} =$

10. $\frac{1}{8} + \frac{6}{8} =$

11. $\frac{4}{9} + \frac{4}{9} =$

12. $\frac{7}{10} + \frac{6}{10} =$

13. $\frac{1}{4} + \frac{2}{4} =$

14. $\frac{4}{10} + \frac{5}{10} =$

15. $\frac{3}{8} + \frac{3}{8} =$

16. $\frac{2}{8} + \frac{4}{8} =$

17. $\frac{3}{6} + \frac{1}{6} =$

18. $\frac{4}{12} + \frac{5}{12} =$

19. $\frac{2}{8} + \frac{7}{8} =$

20. $\frac{8}{12} + \frac{5}{12} =$

21. $\frac{3}{12} + \frac{8}{12} =$

22. $\frac{3}{10} + \frac{3}{10} =$

23. $\frac{5}{9} + \frac{5}{9} =$

24. $\frac{5}{8} + \frac{7}{8} =$

Circle the abbreviations and titles in these sentences. <u>**Remember:**</u> **Abbreviations are short forms of words and usually begin with capital letters and end with periods.**

1. Dr. Cox is my family doctor.
2. Do you live on Rocksberry Rd.?
3. My teacher's name is Ms. Hansen.
4. On Mon. we are taking a trip to Fort Worth, Tx.
5. Will Mr. Harris teach your Sunday school class?
6. Rick's birthday and mine are both on Feb. 16.

Now write the abbreviations for these words.

7. street _____
8. avenue _____
9. postscript _____
10. Miss _____
11. January _____
12. Thursday _____

13. Vermont _____
14. Tuesday _____
15. Mister _____
16. tablespoon _____
17. circle _____
18. company _____

Choose 4 <u>compound</u> <u>words</u> and illustrate them.

EXAMPLE: <u>drawbridge</u> is <u>draw</u> and <u>bridge</u>.

Here are some to choose from, or you can choose some of your own: billfold, screwdriver, backyard, butterfly, rainbow, supermarket, postman, undertake, windpipe, starfish, basketball.

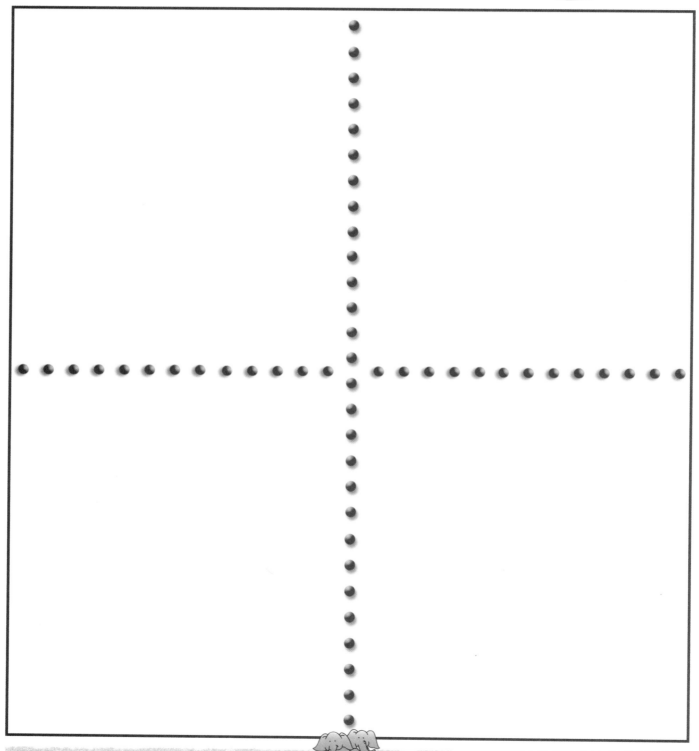

Understanding Polygons.

Closed figures that have straight lines are *polygons*.

Which of these are polygons?_____

Day 18

1.   2.   3.   4.   5.

Why? _____

Where each side or point meets is called a *vertex*. Count and write the number of sides and the number of vertices each polygon has.

    triangle   pentagon   quadrilateral   octagon
sides _____   sides _____   sides _____   sides _____
vertices _____ vertices _____ vertices _____ vertices _____

How are these shapes below alike? _____

How are they different? _____

Write the book titles correctly. <u>Remember</u>: Underline the whole title and use capital letters at the beginning of all the important words and the last word in the title.

1. millions of cats _____

2. higher than the arrow _____

3. john paul jones _____

4. god is in the small stuff _____

5. ludo and the star horse _____

6. marvin k. mooney, will you please go now?

_____

7. an elephant is not a cat _____

8. one wide river to cross _____

9. the polar express _____

10. where the sidewalk ends _____

  71

Neighborhood Survey. Conduct a survey with your neighborhood, friends, or relatives. Find out how many have pets. If possible, observe them with their pets. Do they keep their pets inside or outside? Are the pets left to find their own food, part of their food, or is their food provided for them? How much space do they have to move around in? In what condition are their pets? Think of other questions you might ask. Record your information in a report, chart, graph, table, or picture.

Use what you know about polygons to make a pattern. Start with one polygon and flip, turn, or slide it to make a pattern.

Day 19

EXAMPLE:

or

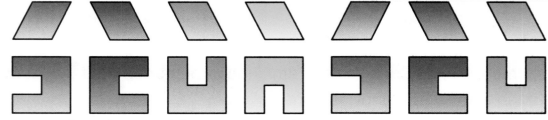

Now try your hand at making some polygon patterns.

• •

Review of Homonyms or Homophones. Write 10 sentences using some of these pairs of homonyms or homophones. Be sure to use both words and underline the homonyms you use.

EXAMPLE: <u>Would</u> you chop some <u>wood</u>?

1. no, know	**7.** sun, son	**13.** rode, road
2. ate, eight	**8.** tail, tale	**14.** pair, pear
3. see, sea	**9.** sale, sail	**15.** their, there
4. knight, night	**10.** so, sew	**16.** hour, our
5. new, knew	**11.** way, weigh	**17.** red, read
6. four, for	**12.** sent, cent	**18.** wear, where

_____

_____

_____

_____

_____

_____

_____

_____

_____

_____

Read this paragraph. Put in the punctuation marks that are missing. Don't forget capitals.

do you ever wonder about the planet pluto it takes pluto 248 earth years to orbit the sun most of the time pluto is farther away from the sun than any other planet but for some time pluto had been closer to the sun than neptune because it was traveling inside neptune's orbit it remained in neptunes orbit until february 9 1999 pluto is now traveling out of neptunes orbit

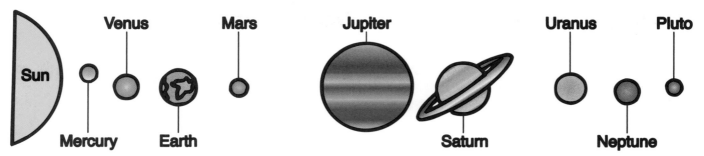

See if you can find more information about Pluto. Did you know that some astronomers believe that it was once a moon of Neptune? Look in an encyclopedia to find out more.

Chart the weather and temperature for the month. You will need to check with the weatherman for the high and low temperatures for the day. Write down or draw the weather for the day. Include the high and low temperature.

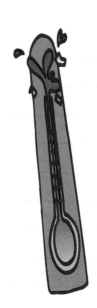

Sun.	Mon.	Tues.	Weds.	Thurs.	Fri.	Sat.

Rename these fractions.
The first one is done for you.

Acts 3:16
By faith in the name of Jesus, this man whom you see and know was made strong...

Day
20

1. $\dfrac{5}{4}$ = $1\dfrac{1}{4}$ 2. $\dfrac{10}{3}$ =   3. $\dfrac{9}{8}$ =   4. $\dfrac{8}{3}$ =

5. $\dfrac{5}{2}$ =   6. $\dfrac{7}{4}$ =   7. $\dfrac{10}{3}$ =   8. $\dfrac{11}{10}$ =

9. $\dfrac{10}{7}$ =   10. $\dfrac{19}{8}$ =   11. $\dfrac{25}{10}$ =   12. $\dfrac{9}{5}$ =

13. $\dfrac{31}{10}$ =   14. $\dfrac{23}{10}$ =   15. $\dfrac{17}{8}$ =   16. $\dfrac{13}{3}$ =

17. $\dfrac{25}{12}$ =   18. $\dfrac{28}{9}$ =   19. $\dfrac{36}{10}$ =   20. $\dfrac{9}{4}$ =

21. $\dfrac{13}{6}$ =   22. $\dfrac{215}{100}$ =   23. $\dfrac{76}{25}$ =   24. $\dfrac{100}{3}$ =

Name the parts of a letter.

 _____

2 _____

3 _____

4 _____

5 _____

1 ⎰ 1624 Oak Avenue
   ⎱ Amarillo, TX 79103
   June 20, 1995

2 {Dear Patt,

Today my friends and I went to Vacation Bible School. We had a lot of fun.
    I sure miss you. I wish your family hadn't moved. Have you made any new friends yet?
    Please write to me as soon as you can.

4 {Your friend,
    {Judy

5

Complete each sentence by circling the word that is spelled correctly, then write it in the blank space. Use a dictionary if necessary.

1. Shadrach, Meshach, and Abednego were able to _____ from harm.
   a. escape   b. iscape   c. eskape   d. acape   e. iccape

2. Mother paid $100.00 for _____.
   a. groseries   b. groceeries   c. groceries   d. grcerees   e. grooseries

3. Anna is a very _____ person.
   a. kreative   b. creative   c. createive   d. crative   e. creetive

4. Have you ever seen a more _____ man?
   a. handsum   b. hansome   c. handsume   d. handcome   e. handsome

5. We love to _____ ride in the winter.
   a. sleigh   b. sleia   c. cleigh   d. slagh   e. sleeigh

6. I found the perfect _____ for my new dress.
   a. matterial   b. matirial   c. metariel   d. material   e. materiall

7. Scott's son got a _____ to Harvard University.
   a. schoolarship   b. scholarship   c. skullarship   d. sholarship   e. scholership

8. What would it take to _____ your appetite?
   a. satesfy   b. satisfi   c. satisffy   d. catisfy   e. satisfy

9. Richard, turn down the _____!
   a. volime   b. volumee   c. volume   d. volumme   e. valume

10. That was a _____ report, Amy.
    a. fantistic   b. fantastik   c. fanntastic   d. fantastic   e. fantestic

11. We saw a man fight an _____ in the show.
    a. aligator   b. alligator   c. allegator   d. alligetor   e. alligater

12. Do you understand the _____?
    a. instructions   b. enstructions   c. instiructions   d. instrucions   e. instracteons

***Electricity.* Make a list of all the things around you that use electricity.**

_____

_____

_____

_____

_____

_____

_____

_____

_____

_____

_____

Words to Sound, Read, and Spell

ability
capability

accept
except

adapt
adept
adopt

adjoin
adjourn

advice
advise

affect
effect

aid
aide

air
heir

all right
alright

all together
altogether

allusion
illusion

although
though

appraise
apprise

arms
alms

ascent
assent

assay
essay

averse
adverse

bases
basis

beau
bough
bow

bell
belle

beside
besides

born
borne

bullion
bouillon

breach
breech

calendar
calender

callous
callus

cannon
canon

canvass
canvas

capital
capitol

casual
causal

sensor
censure

cents
scents
sense

cession
session

charted
charter

choral
coral
corral

cite
sight
site

clench
clinch

flick
clique

coarse
course

complement
compliment

compose
comprise

confidant
confident

core
corps

council
counsel

continual
continuous

coward
cowered

currant
current

decree
degree

defer
differ

descent
dissent

desert
dessert

distract
detract

emigrate
immigrate

eminent
imminent

ensure
insure

envelop
envelope

errand
errant

exalt
exult

extant
extent

fair
fare

farther
further

feint
faint

flair
flare

flew
flu
flue

flounder
founder

flout
flaunt

foreword
forward

formally
formerly

frees
freeze
frieze

gait
gate

grate
great

grisly
gristly
grizzly

hail
hale

hallow
hollow

hangar
hanger

hoard
horde

hoarse
horse

Words to Sound, Read, and Spell

hospitable
hospital

idle
idol

incite
insight

intense
intents

interstate
intrastate
intestate

its
it's

jam
jamb

key
quay
cay

kneed
need

knight
night

later
latter

lay
lie

lean
lien

leave
let

lend
loan

liable
libel

load
lode

loath
loathe

lose
loose

main
mane

manner
manor

mantel
mantle

maybe
may be

medal
mettle

moat
mote

morning
mourning

naval
navel

ordinance
ordnance

pail
pale

pain
pane

palate
palette
pallet

passed
past

peak
peek
pique

peddle
pedal

peer
pier

personal
personnel

plane
plain

pole
pull

pore
pour
poor

pray
prey

prescribe
proscribe

pretense
pretext

rain
reign
rein

raise
raze

respectfully
respectively

role
roll

root
route

sail
sale

set
sit

shear
sheer

sloe
slough
slow

soar
sore

speciality
specialty

stationary
stationery

straight
strait

tail
tale

team
teem

tear
tier

tenant
tenet

then
than

their
there
they're

tic
tick

timber
timbre

track
tract

vail
vale

vain
vane

vial
vile

waive
wave

weather
whether

were
was

wet
whet

whither
wither

who
whom

who's
whose

wrack
rack

wrest
rest

Motivational Calendar!

Month _____

My parents and I decided that if I complete 15 days of
Summer Bridge Activities™ for Young Christians and
read _____ minutes a day, my incentive/reward will be:

_____

Child's Signature _____ Parent's Signature _____

Day 1 ☆ 🕊 📖 _____   Day 9 ☆ 🕊 📖 _____

Day 2 ☆ 🕊 📖 _____   Day 10 ☆ 🕊 📖 _____

Day 3 ☆ 🕊 📖 _____   Day 11 ☆ 🕊 📖 _____

Day 4 ☆ 🕊 📖 _____   Day 12 ☆ 🕊 📖 _____

Day 5 ☆ 🕊 📖 _____   Day 13 ☆ 🕊 📖 _____

Day 6 ☆ 🕊 📖 _____   Day 14 ☆ 🕊 📖 _____

Day 7 ☆ 🕊 📖 _____   Day 15 ☆ 🕊 📖 _____

Day 8 ☆ 🕊 📖 _____

Child: Color the ☆ for daily activities completed.
Color the 🕊 for daily devotionals completed.
Color the 📖 for daily reading completed.

Parent: Initial the _____ when all activities are complete.

Jesus loves me!

Discover Something New!

Fun Activity Ideas to Go Along with the Third Section!

1. Draw a picture of your favorite friend, toy, or teacher during your favorite time of the year.

2. Put together a collection of leaves from your neighborhood and label as many as you can.

3. Write five questions that you would like to ask the president of the United States.

4. Invent a new ice cream flavor. How is it made? What will you call it?

5. Play football with a Frisbee.

6. Find out how to recycle in your town; then make and deliver flyers to inform all your neighbors.

7. Using a book on astronomy, look for stars and constellations. This is a fun nighttime activity.

8. Write your answer to the following question: How would the world be different without Alexander Graham Bell?

9. Surprise your parents and weed a flower bed or garden, rake the leaves, do the dishes, etc.

10. Play flashlight tag, tonight!

11. Design a comic strip and draw it.

12. Paint a mural on butcher paper.

13. Pretend you live in the year 2028. How will life be different? How will you look? What will you eat? How will you get around? Write it down and draw it.

14. Set up a miniature golf course in your own backyard.

15. Play hockey using a broom.

Add and rename fractions where needed. The first one is done for you.

Day 1

1. $\frac{3}{4} + \frac{2}{4} = \frac{5}{4}$ or $1\frac{1}{4}$

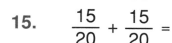

2. $\frac{9}{11} + \frac{2}{11} =$

3. $\frac{7}{12} + \frac{8}{12} =$

4. $\frac{9}{16} + \frac{9}{16} =$

5. $\frac{6}{10} + \frac{8}{10} =$

6. $\frac{10}{12} + \frac{14}{12} =$

7. $\frac{5}{10} + \frac{6}{10} =$

8. $\frac{12}{24} + \frac{13}{24} =$

9. $\frac{4}{7} + \frac{5}{7} =$

10. $\frac{3}{4} + \frac{5}{4} =$

11. $\frac{6}{11} + \frac{7}{11} =$

12. $\frac{5}{15} + \frac{10}{15} =$

13. $\frac{8}{9} + \frac{6}{9} =$

14. $\frac{10}{16} + \frac{9}{16} =$

15. $\frac{15}{20} + \frac{15}{20} =$

Look at the the letter on page 75 to answer the following questions.

1. What does the heading tell you? _____

_____

2. How many paragraphs are in the letter? _____

3. What is the signature? _____

_____

4. What words in the letter have capitals? _____

_____

_____

5. Where are the commas in the letter? _____

_____

_____

_____

_____

  81

Electric Circuit Crossword Puzzle.

Across

1. Electric currents from a battery flow in one direction from
n __ __ __ __ __ __ __ to p __ __ __ __ __ __ __.

2. Electrical c __ __ __ __ __ __ means the flow of charged particles.

3. M __ __ __ __ __ are good conductors of electrical currents because electricity can flow through them easily.

4. The plastic or rubber coverings on wires are called i __ __ __ __ __ __ __ __ __ __.

5. In a lightbulb, when the switch is turned on or connected, the electricity flows through what we call a c __ __ __ __ __ c __ __ __ __ __ __.

6. When electricity flows through the wires on a toaster they become hot, and h __ __ __ from the wires toasts our bread.

7. L __ __ __ __ __ and thickness are the two things that determine the wires' resistance that causes them to become hot.

8. A __ __ __ __ __ __ __ __ __ such as electric stoves and toasters contain wires that are conductors of electricity.

9. A b __ __ __ __ __ __ is a cell storing an electrical charge and capable of furnishing an electrical current.

10. Copper and aluminum are good c __ __ __ __ __ __ __ __ __ of electricity because electricity can go through them easily due to their low resistance to the electrical current.

Down

1. A r __ __ __ __ __ __ __ __ is a tool used to control the amount of electrical current that goes through a circuit.

2. When wires, bulbs, and batteries are connected they make a path for electricity to flow through called an
e __ __ __ __ __ __ __ __ __
c __ __ __ __ __ __ __.

3. Lightbulbs have a special wire in them called a
f __ __ __ __ __ __ __.

4. The property of the filament that makes it light up when electricity flows through it is called the
r __ __ __ __ __ __ __ __ __ __
to electricity.

Subtracting Fractions.

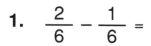

$$\frac{4}{5} - \frac{1}{5} = \frac{3}{5}$$ ← subtract the numerators
← keep the same denominators

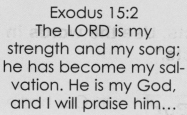

Day **2**

1. $\dfrac{2}{6} - \dfrac{1}{6} =$

2. $\dfrac{5}{10} - \dfrac{3}{10} =$

3. $\dfrac{3}{4} - \dfrac{2}{4} =$

4. $\dfrac{6}{8} - \dfrac{3}{8} =$

5. $\dfrac{8}{11} - \dfrac{3}{11} =$

6. $\dfrac{6}{7} - \dfrac{4}{7} =$

7. $\dfrac{11}{12} - \dfrac{7}{12} =$

8. $\dfrac{4}{5} - \dfrac{1}{5} =$

9. $\dfrac{5}{9} - \dfrac{2}{9} =$

10. $6\dfrac{8}{10}$
$-3\dfrac{4}{10}$

11. $8\dfrac{4}{10}$
$-3\dfrac{3}{10}$

12. $7\dfrac{2}{5}$
$-3\dfrac{1}{5}$

13. $6\dfrac{7}{8}$
$-3\dfrac{4}{8}$

14. $13\dfrac{3}{4}$
$-9\dfrac{1}{4}$

15. $14\dfrac{10}{12}$
$-7\dfrac{9}{12}$

16. $24\dfrac{7}{10}$
$-12\dfrac{3}{10}$

17. $15\dfrac{8}{9}$
$-7\dfrac{3}{9}$

Put all the punctuation marks and capital letters in this letter.

Mr. Greg Jones
1461 Condor St.
Lake Tona, OH

1461 condor st
lake tona oh
july 21 1995

dear david

thank you for sending me the pictures of your trip it looks like you had a great time do you want me to send them back

next week im going to kansas city to spend the rest of the summer with my dad i hope we will get along well

write again when you can

your friend

greg

Body Facts. Use the words in the Word Box to complete these sentences on "body facts."

Word Box

- brain
- water
- calcium
- circulatory
- cells
- iron
- digestive
- eyes
- heart

1. Our bodies are made up of millions of tiny _____.

2. Our bodies are mostly _____, between 55 and 75 percent.

3. Our bodies have lots of metals and minerals in them, some of which are _____ and _____.

4. Our bodies have several systems that work together to help us. Our heart, blood vessels, and blood are part of our _____ system, which moves blood throughout our bodies.

5. Our salivary glands, esophagus, stomach, gallbladder, large intestines, and small intestines are part of our _____ system.

6. Our _____ is like a wonderful tool. It tells our _____ to beat and our _____ to blink.

Our Five Senses Can Sense Danger! Think about your five senses—touch, smell, sight, hearing, and taste. Now list all the ways your five senses can protect you or keep you from danger. Which sense do you trust most to keep you from danger?

_____

_____

_____

_____

_____

_____

_____

_____

_____

_____

Addition and Subtraction with Thousands

Exodus 15:13
"In your unfailing love you will lead the people you have redeemed..."

Day 3

1. 5,162
− 2,678

2. 9,252
− 5,003

3. 7,825
− 3,148

5. 8,929
+ 4,050

6. 9,341
− 6,037

7. 2,629
+ 7,536

8. 4,528
+ 1,257

9. 7,932
− 5,847

10. 9,826
+ 1,329

11. 4,723
+ 5,297

12. 3,872
− 1,799

13. 8,000
− 4,587

14. 7,909
+ 5,360

15. 9,031
− 5,592

16. 2,354
+ 5,967

Write a letter of encouragement to someone in need of prayer. Be sure to put in all five parts of the letter. <u>Remember</u>: Letter writing uses the same steps as writing a story. Refer to page 59. Copy your letter to another sheet of paper.

Below are the stressed syllables of some spelling words. Write the other syllables and then write the words in cursive. Each blank stands for a letter. The first one is done for you.

favor	amount	busy	accept	violin
paddle	piano	begin	dial	bacon
several	salad	wonderful	unlock	vegetable
~~parent~~	library	limit	into	depend

1. par´ _ent_   _parent_
2. li´ _ _ _ _ _   _____
3. lim´ _ _   _____
4. in´ _ _   _____
5. _ _ pend´   _____
6. ba´ _ _ _   _____
7. di´ _ _   _____
8. _ _ gin´   _____
9. _ _ a´ _ _   _____
10. pad´ _ _ _   _____

11. sev´ _ _ _ _   _____
12. sal´ _ _   _____
13. won´ _ _ _ _ _   _____
14. _ _ lock´   _____
15. veg´ _ _ _ _ _ _   _____
16. _ _ _ lin´   _____
17. _ _ cept´   _____
18. bus´ _   _____
19. _ mount´   _____
20. fa´ _ _ _   _____

Self-Portrait Poem.

1. Write your name.
2. Write two words that tell about you.
3. Write three words that tell what you like to do.
4. Write two more words that describe you.
5. Write your name again.

Try writing another "portrait poem" about a favorite person or pet in your life.

_____   _____
_____   _____
_____   _____
_____   _____
_____   _____
_____   _____
_____   _____

It's about Time! Remember: There are 24 hours in a day. The times from midnight to noon are written a.m., and the times from noon to midnight are written p.m. Write down the times. Remember a.m. and p.m.

Day
4

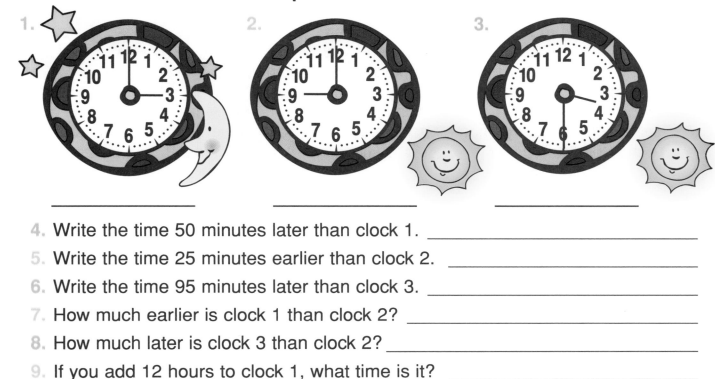

1. _____
2. _____
3. _____

4. Write the time 50 minutes later than clock 1. _____

5. Write the time 25 minutes earlier than clock 2. _____

6. Write the time 95 minutes later than clock 3. _____

7. How much earlier is clock 1 than clock 2? _____

8. How much later is clock 3 than clock 2? _____

9. If you add 12 hours to clock 1, what time is it? _____

10. What was the time 6 hours earlier on clock 2? _____

This envelope is not addressed correctly. Rewrite it correctly. Remember: The return address is the address of the person writing the letter, and the address is the address of the person to whom the letter is going.

1461 condor st
mr greg jones
lake tona oh

mr david fisher
little creek id
route 2 box 3 f

Who Did It?

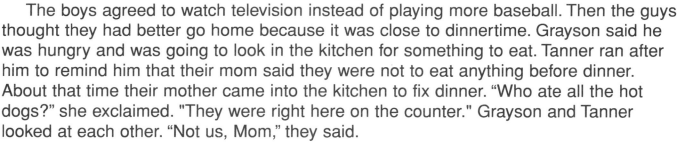

Grayson and Tanner were playing baseball in their backyard with some friends. They had been playing all afternoon in the hot sun.

Tanner decided that he was tired of playing ball. He sat down on the back steps to watch the others. "Man, am I thirsty," he said. "I'm going in the house to get a drink." Several of the others decided that they were thirsty and went inside with Tanner.

"Wait for me!" hollered Grayson. "I'm coming, too!"

The boys agreed to watch television instead of playing more baseball. Then the guys thought they had better go home because it was close to dinnertime. Grayson said he was hungry and was going to look in the kitchen for something to eat. Tanner ran after him to remind him that their mom said they were not to eat anything before dinner. About that time their mother came into the kitchen to fix dinner. "Who ate all the hot dogs?" she exclaimed. "They were right here on the counter." Grayson and Tanner looked at each other. "Not us, Mom," they said.

"Somebody must have. Do you have any clues?"

They started looking around for clues. The mud off their shoes had left tracks on the floor but had come nowhere near where Mother had put the hot dogs. After their survey of the kitchen, they sat down to discuss the "case of the missing hot dogs." Then they heard what sounded like a satisfied meow from the den. The three of them walked into the den to find Tiger, their cat, finishing off the last hot dog. He licked both his paws clean and meowed loudly. "No wonder we didn't find any cat tracks in the kitchen where the hot dogs were," laughed Mother. "Tiger always keeps his paws very clean, unlike some boys I know."

● ●

After reading this story, write down at least five things you know about Tanner and Grayson.

1._____

_____

2._____

_____

3._____

_____

4._____

_____

5._____

_____

Fractions to Tenths and the Decimal Equivalents for the Fraction. <u>Remember</u>: When working with fractions that have a denominator of 10, you can write them as fractions in tenths, or you can use the decimal equivalent. Do this activity by writing each both ways.

1. 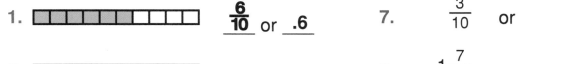 $\frac{6}{10}$ or .6

2. ___ or ___

3. ___ or ___

4. ___ or ___

5. ___ or ___

6. ___ or ___

7. $\frac{3}{10}$ or ___.___

8. $1\frac{7}{10}$ or ___.___

9. $3\frac{5}{10}$ or ___.___

10. 1.9 or _____

11. .8 or _____

12. 3.4 or _____

On page 85, you wrote a letter to someone. Today, address an envelope and send the letter to them. Be sure to put your address in the upper left-hand corner and the address of the person to whom you're sending the letter in the center. Don't forget to put a stamp in the upper right-hand corner. Use the space below to practice.

Write an analogy to finish these sentences. Remember: An analogy is a comparison between two pairs of words. Try to think of the relationship between the two words given and then think of another word that has the same kind of relationship to the third word.

EXAMPLE: Story is to read as song is to sing.

1. Brother is to boy as sister is to _____.

2. Princess is to queen as prince is to _____.

3. Milk is to drink as hamburger is to _____.

4. Arrow is to bow as bullet is to _____.

5. Car is to driver as plane is to _____.

6. Ceiling is to room as lid is to _____.

7. Paper is to tear as glass is to _____.

8. Large is to huge as small is to _____.

9. Wrist is to hand as ankle is to _____.

10. God is to Jesus as father is to _____.

11. Cupboard is to dishes as library is to _____.

12. Hard is to difficult as easy is to _____.

13. Moon is to earth as earth is to _____.

14. Time is to clock as date is to _____.

Exercising Parts of the Body. Make a list of 5 or 6 exercises. Some examples are running, hopping, sit-ups, jumping jacks, touching your toes, push-ups, jumping, skipping, playing sports, gymnastics, and swinging your arms. Try them. Which parts of the body are affected? Write down the results. Try this exercise. Take an ordinary spring-centered clothespin. Hold the ends between your thumb and one of your fingers. How many times can you open and close it in 30 to 40 seconds?

_____

_____

_____

_____

_____

_____

_____

_____

Use what you know about <u>fractions</u> <u>to</u> <u>tenths</u> and their <u>decimal</u> <u>equivalents</u> to work with <u>hundreds</u>. **Remember:** When a whole object is divided into 100 equal parts, each part is <u>one</u> <u>hundredth</u> (¹⁄₁₀₀ or .01). Write the fraction as a decimal.

2 Samuel 22:33
It is God who arms me
with strength and
makes my way perfect.

Day
6

1. $\frac{49}{100}$ = .**49**　　2. $\frac{25}{100}$ = .___　　3. $\frac{20}{100}$ = .___　　4. $\frac{52}{100}$ = .___

5. $\frac{86}{100}$ = .___　　6. $\frac{37}{100}$ = .___　　7. $\frac{4}{100}$ = .___　　8. $\frac{9}{100}$ = .___

Now write the mixed number as a decimal.

9. $1\frac{93}{100}$ = __.__　　10. $7\frac{15}{100}$ = __.__　　11. $9\frac{13}{100}$ = __.__　　12. $15\frac{47}{100}$ = __.__

13. $46\frac{89}{100}$ = __.__　　14. $35\frac{6}{100}$ = __.__　　15. $94\frac{7}{100}$ = __.__　　16. $625\frac{12}{100}$ = __.__

17. $12\frac{5}{100}$ = __.__　　18. $81\frac{1}{100}$ = __.__　　19. $37\frac{87}{100}$ = __.__　　20. $10\frac{11}{100}$ = __.__

Adjectives are words that tell about or describe nouns and pronouns. Circle the adjective(s) in these sentences. Write the noun(s) or pronoun(s) described at the end of the sentence. The first one is done for you.

1. A (beautiful) light flashed across the (cloudy) sky. _light_　　_sky_

2. Her golden hair was very long. _____

3. On the tall mountain we found blue and yellow flowers. _____

_____

4. Daniel was brave while he was in the lions' den. _____

5. It is fun, but it is also dangerous to skydive. _____

6. Our brown dog had six cute puppies. _____

_____

Now fill in the blanks with adjectives.

7. My _____ pencil is never in my desk.

8. The _____ students were having a _____ time.

9. Lions are _____ animals that we can see in the zoo.

10. The _____, _____ ride was making me sick.

11. My brother, Jack, sang a _____ song when we were camping.

12. _____, _____ snakes were wiggling around in the box.

Maintaining Good Health. Fill in the blanks with the following health terms: nutrients, healthy, sleep, exercise, liquids, water, cleanliness, checkups, energy, food groups.

1. _____ are basic nourishing ingredients in good foods that we eat.
2. _____ helps us to strengthen our muscles. It helps our heart and lungs grow, too.
3. _____ help us prevent tooth decay and maintain good health.
4. Meat, fruits and vegetables, milk, and breads and cereals make up the basic four _____ _____ that keep us healthy.
5. Being healthy means feeling good and having the _____ to work and play.
6. Vitamins and minerals are kinds of _____ that we get from food.
7. Being _____ means feeling good and not being sick.
8. Sugar, starch, and fats are _____ that the body uses for fuel to give us _____.
9. We need to drink a lot of _____ because our body is approximately 55–75% _____.
10. Plenty of _____ helps give our body time to grow and repair itself. Children need 10 to 11 hours of it because they are not finished growing.
11. _____ is a way of fighting germs and staying healthy.
12. We need health _____ by a doctor or dentist at least once a year.

Are You Confused?

1. Are any of the lines curved?

_____

2. Which line is the longest?

_____

3. Which vase is wider at the top and bottom? _____

4. Which line is longer, a or b?

_____

a.

b.

5. Is the hat taller than it is wide? _____

Decimals and Money.
Remember: 100 pennies = 1 dollar.
One penny is 1/100 of a dollar, or $.01, so 49 pennies = $.49. We can compute money by adding, subtracting, multiplying, and dividing—just watch the decimals. Look at the signs. Use a separate piece of paper to show your work.

Day 7

EXAMPLE:

```
  $57.34
+ 62.89
 $120.23
```

```
  $62.89
- 34.91
  $27.98
```

```
  $12.45
x      3
  $37.35
```

```
        $3.95
   5 ) $19.75
       -15
        47
       -45
        25
       -25
         0
```

1.
```
  $409.75
- 249.83
  $   .
```

2.
```
  $14.74
x      3
  $   .
```

3.
```
  $492.00
- 349.50
  $   .
```

4.
```
        $   .
   4 ) $12.92
```

5.
```
  $162.49
+ 186.32
  $   .
```

6.
```
        $    .
   7 ) $49.77
```

7.
```
  $601.89
+ 403.23
  $   .
```

8.
```
  $9.57
x    6
$   .
```

9.
```
  $668.45
+ 171.63
  $   .
```

10.
```
  $915.04
- 102.56
  $   .
```

11.
```
  $741.13
x      8
  $   .
```

12.
```
        $   .
   4 ) $29.48
```

Write nouns to go with these adjectives. The first one is done for you.

1. two, red _apples_
2. fluffy, yellow _____
3. cold, wet _____
4. dark, strange _____
5. wild, dangerous _____
6. black, furry _____
7. big, heavy _____
8. fancy, little _____

9. pink, small _____
10. smooth, green _____
11. fat, juicy _____
12. loud, shrill _____
13. fourteen, blue _____
14. long, thick _____
15. cozy, warm _____
16. sharp, silver _____

93 © Summer Bridge Activities™ 4–5

Add a prefix and a suffix to the following words; then choose five of the words and write a sentence with them.

prefix

suffix

1. _____ print _____
2. _____ light _____
3. _____ poison _____
4. _____ courage_____
5. _____agree _____
6. _____spell _____

7. _____lock _____
8. _____port _____
9. _____ cook _____
10. _____ appoint _____
11. _____ record _____
12. _____ health _____

Sentences:

1. _____
_____

2. _____
_____

3. _____
_____

4. _____
_____

5. _____
_____

What's for Breakfast, Lunch, and Dinner? This is your day to plan the meals. You can have anything you want to eat for the day. It can be for the whole family or just yourself. Plan and write down your menu for breakfast, lunch, and dinner. You can even schedule a few snacks.

_____
_____
_____
_____
_____
_____
_____
_____
_____
_____

Multiplying Multiples of 10 and 100. To use shortcuts to find the product of multiples of 10 or 100, write the product for the basic fact and count the zeros in the factors.

1 Chronicles 16:11
Look to the LORD and his strength; seek his face always.

10 x 8 = 80 (1 zero) 10 x 80 = 800 (2 zeros) 10 x 800 = 8,000 (3 zeros)

Multiples of tens:

1. 10 x 5 = _____   2. 7 x 10 = _____   3. 39 x 10 = _____

4. 30 x 30 = _____   5. 54 x 10 = _____   6. 10 x 21 = _____

7. 710 x 10 = _____   8. 9 x 10 = _____   9. 70 x 30 = _____

10. 40 x 40 = _____   11. 85 x 10 = _____   12. 341 x 10 = _____

Multiples of hundreds:

13. 900   14. 600   15. 230   16. 700
    x 40   x 10   x 20   x 80

17. 500   18. 600   19. 440   20. 700
    x 50   x 90   x30   x 60

Adjectives can be used to compare. Write these adjectives. Add -er and -est.

EXAMPLE: red _____ *redder* _____ *reddest* _____

1. hot _____ _____ _____

2. nice _____ _____ _____

3. warm _____ _____ _____

4. hard _____ _____ _____

5. easy _____ _____ _____

6. few _____ _____ _____

Now retell a Bible story. Use as many of the adjectives above as you can. Underline the adjectives.

_____

_____

_____

_____

_____

_____

Idioms. Choose 4 <u>idioms and illustrate them</u>. Here are some to choose from, or you can use your own.

- Lend a hand.
- She's a ball of fire.
- He's got rocks in his head.
- She gave him a dirty look.
- I got it straight from the horse's mouth.
- You won the game by the skin of your teeth.

- Time flies.
- Keep a stiff upper lip.
- The boys were shooting the breeze.
- I'd really like to catch her eye.
- I was dog tired.

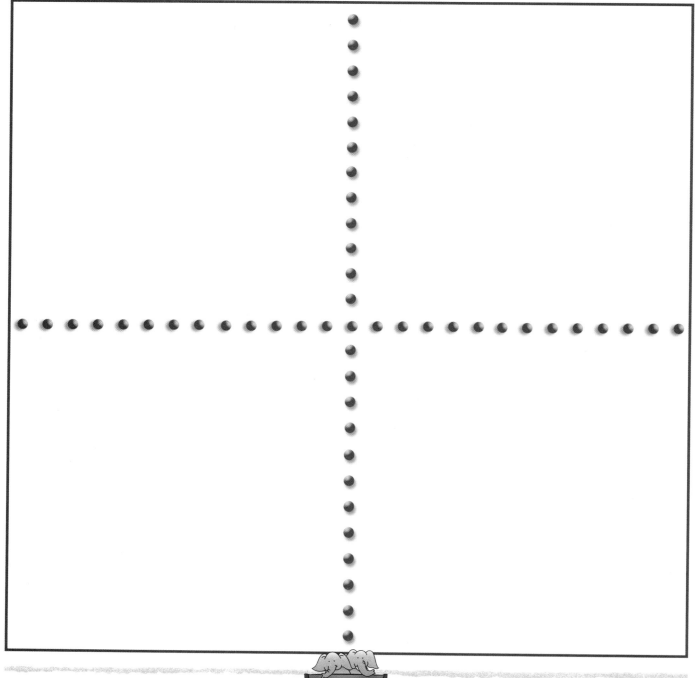

Place Value. A place-value chart can help us read as well as figure out large numbers.

Eleanor Roosevelt: You gain strength, courage, and confidence by...[doing] the thing you think you cannot do.

Day 9

Hundred Millions	Ten Millions	Millions	Hundred Thousands	Ten Thousands	Thousands	Hundreds	Tens	Ones
	8	6	5	3	7	1	4	3

Using the place-value chart to help you, read and write the following numbers. The first one is done for you.

1. Eighty-six million five hundred thirty-seven thousand one hundred forty-three __86,537,143__.

2. Seven hundred eighty-nine million four hundred ninety-six thousand three hundred twenty-one _____.

3. One hundred sixty million seven hundred six thousand one hundred twenty-nine _____.

4. Seventy-one million four hundred eleven thousand eight hundred ninety-nine _____.

5. One hundred million three hundred seventy-five thousand _____.

6. Ninety million two hundred fifty-seven thousand four hundred forty-three _____.

7. 1,369,000 _____

8. 375,403,101 _____

9. 894,336,045 _____

10. 284,300,070 _____

Overworked <u>And.</u> **Rewrite the paragraph <u>and</u> leave out all the occurrences of <u>and</u> that you can. Write in cursive <u>and</u> be sure to put capitals <u>and</u> periods where they need to go.**

My friend and I visited Cardiff, Wales, and we learned that Cardiff is the capital and largest port of Wales and the city lies on the River Taff near the Bristol Channel and Cardiff is near the largest coal mines in Great Britain and it is one of the great coal-shipping ports of the world.

_____
_____
_____
_____

How many times were you able to leave <u>and</u> out of the paragraph? _____

The following words are often misspelled. Write each word three times; then have someone give you a test. Use another piece of paper for your test.

EXAMPLE:

1. although _____ *although* _____ *although* _____ *although* _____
2. arithmetic _____
3. trouble _____
4. bought _____
5. chocolate _____
6. aunt _____
7. handkerchief _____
8. piece _____
9. vacation _____
10. practice _____
11. receive _____
12. getting _____
13. lessons _____
14. weather _____
15. surprise _____

YOUR Test Score

Categorizing the People in Your Family. Include some aunts, uncles, and cousins. Categorize them according to age, height, weight, hair color, hair length, eye color, etc. What do they have in common? What are some of their differences? Then draw a picture of them. Use another sheet of paper.

family member	age	height	weight	hair color

Multiplying 2-Digit Numbers.

Day 10

1. 39
    x 69

2. 72
    x 18

3. 85
    x 36

4. 46
    x 77

5. 57
    x 49

6. 41
    x 73

7. 48
    x 95

8. 88
    x 66

9. 68
    x 92

10. 507
    x 13

11. 456
    x 32

12. 640
    x 21

13. 576
    x 45

● ●

Write S behind the word pairs that are synonyms, A for antonyms, or H for homonyms.

EXAMPLE:
tie • bind __S__
high • low __A__
here • hear __H__

1. weep • cry _____
2. wonderful • terrible _____
3. look • glare _____
4. huge • large _____
5. away • toward _____
6. walk • stroll _____
7. never • always _____
8. bear • bare _____
9. ask • told _____
10. cymbal • symbol _____
11. many • numerous _____
12. end • begin _____

13. hair • hare _____
14. move • transport _____
15. problem • solution _____
16. idea • thought _____
17. claws • clause _____
18. I'll • isle _____
19. add • subtract _____
20. try • attempt _____
21. that • this _____
22. doe • dough _____
23. enough • ample _____
24. board • bored _____
25. day • date _____
26. capital • capitol _____
27. leave • arrive _____

Do this crossword puzzle. Read the clues to help you decide what words go in the boxes.

Down

1. birds with webbed feet
3. plays the piano
5. gave money
6. holds up the gate
8. boards for building
9. frilly
11. do it again to a story
12. hair by the eye
13. carried Jesus at Passover

Across

2. red from the sun
4. won't bend easily
5. eat outside
6. beginning of a word
7. decay of food
10. very large; great
14. nothing in it
15. cook in

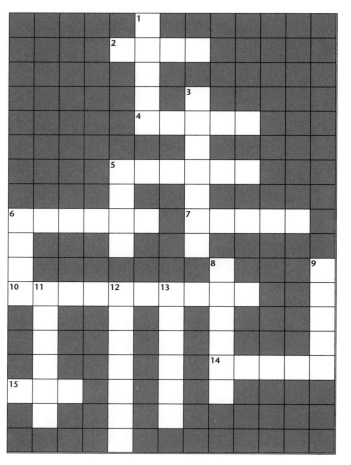

Finish drawing the illusion. Is it a face or a vase? It's both! (Look until you see them.)

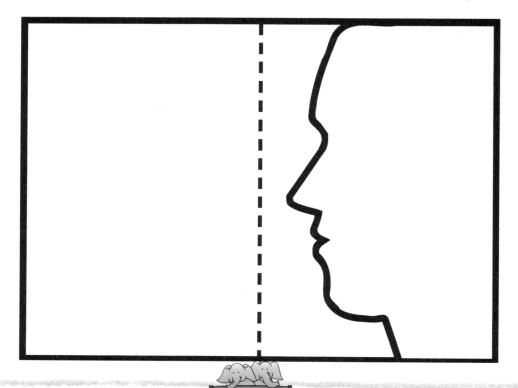

Quotients with Remainders.
Use another sheet of paper if you need to.

EXAMPLE:

1. $20\overline{)48}$ **2 R8**
    $\underline{40}$
    8

2. $30\overline{)189}$

3. $70\overline{)456}$

4. $80\overline{)504}$

5. $30\overline{)281}$

6. $60\overline{)246}$

7. $90\overline{)458}$

8. $60\overline{)573}$

9. $40\overline{)172}$

10. $30\overline{)216}$

11. $30\overline{)121}$

12. $90\overline{)500}$

13. $80\overline{)410}$

12. $60\overline{)692}$

15. $70\overline{)661}$

Think of one of your favorite Bible stories. Tell how the story begins, what happens in the middle, and how it ends. Write it in your own words and in the correct order. Don't write the whole story.

Categorize these words and tell why they go in the same category. You put the headings in this time.

deciliter	program	kindness	remorse	softball
quart	soccer	yard	hate	acre
anger	software	jealousy	Fahrenheit	joystick
swimming	Celsius	liter	ton	gram
ounce	disk	mouse	cursor	meter
tennis	basketball	rugby	kilogram	fear

1.	2.	3.	4.	5.

Tell why. Because they all…

1. _____

2. _____

3. _____

4. _____

5. _____

Make a "Happy" list and then a "Sad" list. Put the things that make you most happy at the top of your "Happy" list. Do the same thing with things that make you sad on your "Sad" list.

Happy List 😃

Sad List ☹

Multiplying Money. Remember: Multiply as you do using whole numbers and then place the decimal point or cents (2 numbers from the right). **Use another sheet of paper to show your work.**

Day 12

EXAMPLE:

```
  $.24      24  x    9   =   216
  x 89      24  x   80   =  1920
   216     1920  +  216   =  2136
 +1920    Place the decimal and the dollar sign
  2136     $21.36
```

1. $.65
   x 24

2. $.52
   x 36

3. $.94
   x 13

4. $.45
   x 25

5. $.81
   x 34

6. $.59
   x 54

7. $.75
   x 22

8. $.98
   x 34

9. $3.45
   x 56

10. $3.52
    x 34

11. $5.75
    x 24

12. $8.93
    x 73

Adverbs Describe Verbs. Write an adverb to describe these verbs.
Remember: Many adverbs end with -ly. The first one is done for you

1. walk ___*quietly*___

2. smiled _____

3. painted _____

4. laughed _____

5. prayed _____

6. folded _____

7. _____ run

8. _____ looked

9. burned _____

10. _____ cried

11. went _____

12. answered _____

Write five sentences using the verbs and adverbs you put together.

EXAMPLE: I will <u>walk</u> <u>quietly</u> in the library.

13. _____

14. _____

15. _____

16. _____

17. _____

Read a book and fill out the following book report. Share it with a sister, brother, or friend.

Title: _____
_____
Author: _____
Illustrator: _____
Setting (where): _____
_____
Main Characters (who): _____
_____
_____
_____
Main Ideas (what): _____
_____
_____

I liked the book because: _____
_____
_____
_____
_____
_____
_____

Tell which character in the book you would like to be and why:
_____
_____
_____
_____

Dictionary Sentences. Rewrite the following dictionary sentences using the correct spelling.

1. Thaŋk ū fôr thə yel´ō T shûrt and blak shərts.

_____

2. Mis´tẽr Ralf livz ôn ə färm doun əlôŋ thə riv´ẽr.

_____

3. I stak´əd ôl thə kanz ôn top uv ēch uth´ẽr.

_____

4. Wē nēd ə gal´ən uv milk, sum egz, and but´ẽr, nou!

_____

Now rewrite these two sentences using the dictionary.

1. A thousand pennies equal ten dollars, I am told.

_____

2. Monkeys are funny, furry little animals in the zoo.

_____

Geometry. Explain to an adult what the following geometrical terms mean. Show what each means by drawing an example of each.

Psalm 21:1
O LORD, the king rejoices in your strength. How great is his joy in the victories you give!

Day 13

1. Segments, lines, endpoints, and rays

2. Intersecting lines

3. Parallel lines

4. Perimeter

● ●

Adverbs tell <u>where</u>, <u>how</u>, or <u>when</u>. Tell what kind of adverb is underlined in the following sentences. Write <u>where</u>, <u>when</u>, or <u>how</u>.

1. Animals are <u>sometimes</u> called mammals. _____
2. There was a big accident on the freeway <u>yesterday</u>. _____
3. Joe <u>quickly</u> ran out to catch the bus. _____
4. We could hear the sound far <u>below</u> us. _____
5. The wise men followed the <u>brightly</u> shining star. _____
6. We are going <u>there</u> next winter. _____
7. Be sure and write your letter <u>neatly</u>. _____
8. The birds will fly <u>away</u> if you scare them. _____
9. Father is going to leave <u>immediately</u>. _____
10. The baby played <u>happily</u> on the lawn. _____

Where? How? When?

Now fill in the blanks with a <u>how</u>, <u>when</u>, or <u>where</u> adverb.

1. The car was going very (how) _____.
2. Will you take April and June (where) _____ to the movie?
3. Mom will take them down (when) _____.

Add one or two syllables to the words below to make two new words. Make sure you spell the words correctly.

EXAMPLE: low **pillow** **follow**

1. law _____ _____
2. place _____ _____
3. rock _____ _____
4. tire _____ _____
5. band _____ _____
6. bat _____ _____
7. bit _____ _____
8. sent _____ _____
9. sand _____ _____
10. car _____ _____
11. ham _____ _____
12. out _____ _____

13. able _____ _____
14. age _____ _____
15. ten _____ _____
16. man _____ _____
17. cat _____ _____
18. son _____ _____
19. con _____ _____
20. be _____ _____
21. play _____ _____
22. star _____ _____
23. stand _____ _____
24. hob _____ _____

It's important to know what the following words mean, especially when you're taking a test. Circle the letter that gives the best meaning for the underlined word in the sentence.

1. Can you <u>solve</u> this problem?
   a. copy   b. answer   c. recall
2. Make an <u>estimate</u> of how many people are in the U.S.
   a. approximate guess   b. count them   c. rank them
3. Let's take a <u>survey</u> of people who like red licorice.
   a. find out   b. examine   c. select
4. Will you <u>complete</u> your test in ten minutes?
   a. support   b. utilize   c. finish
5. Do <u>sections</u> one and two on this page.
   a. groups   b. parts   c. problems
6. Post office workers <u>classify</u> mail according to locations.
   a. change   b. write   c. arrange or group
7. We were pleased with our <u>survey</u> of the house.
   a. examination   b. explain   c. understanding
8. You will have to <u>prove</u> your answers.
   a. sample   b. question   c. to show as right and true
9. Do you understand the <u>directions</u>?
   a. why   b. describe it   c. how to do
10. Spencer <u>usually</u> knows the right answers.
    a. never   b. always   c. most of the time
11. You have to <u>apply</u> yourself if you want to get good grades.
    a. work and stick to it   b. justify   c. recommend
12. Read the book and <u>summarize</u> it for the class.
    a. reread   b. describe briefly   c. show how

More Geometry. Explain and draw an example of the following geometrical terms.

Rachel Carson: Those who contemplate the beauty of the earth find reserves of strength that will endure as long as life lasts.

Day 14

1. Congruent figures

2. Right angles

3. Triangles

4. Parallelograms

5. Polygons

- -

Sometimes it's fun to share a story with someone else. Read a book, then call one of your friends or go visit them. Tell your friend about the book you read.

Tell who the main characters are. Tell where the story takes place. Tell the plot or main event of the story. But don't tell them how the story ends. See if you can get them to read the book.

On the rest of this page, write what happened. Did you get your friend to read the book?

_____

_____

_____

_____

_____

_____

_____

_____

_____

_____

Create small words from the letters in the following words. Write them. You may find more than one in most words.

EXAMPLE: borrow   *row*   or   *bow*   *rob*

1. pajamas _____
2. carpenter _____
3. performance _____
4. bandage _____
5. knowledge _____
6. theory _____
7. satisfaction _____
8. customer _____
9. discovery _____
10. eventually _____
11. announcement _____
12. creation _____
13. theater _____
14. honorable _____
15. investigate _____

Sometimes things happen that cause something else to happen. This is called "cause and effect." A clue word helps to tell which is which. In the following sentences, underline the cause with a straight line (___). Underline the effect with a dotted line (_ _ _). Put a box ☐ around the clue word. The first one is done for you.

1. The tooth was broken, ☐so☐ it gave her a lot of pain.
2. The book was ripped and dirty because the dog got it.
3. Because it was so cold, Betty could ice skate for only a short while.
4. I went to bed early last night because I was so tired.
5. Since it was raining so hard, we couldn't play outside.
6. The rabbit ran fast because the fox was after it.
7. It was very foggy out, so we could not see the mountains.
8. Because we got to the camp late in the day, there was no time for hiking.
9. It was very dark in the dugout, so we turned on the flashlight.
10. Kit played basketball too long after school; therefore, he missed the bus.
11. Laura's letter was returned because she forgot to put a stamp on it.
12. Mike's suitcase broke when it fell off the car. As a result, he had to put his things in a paper bag.

Graphs, Charts, and Tables. There are many different kinds of graphs, charts, and tables. Check your newspaper regularly to find different kinds and different information that you could chart or graph daily. This is a "broken-line" graph. Complete this graph using the information given in the table. Monday and Tuesday have been done for you.

Day 15

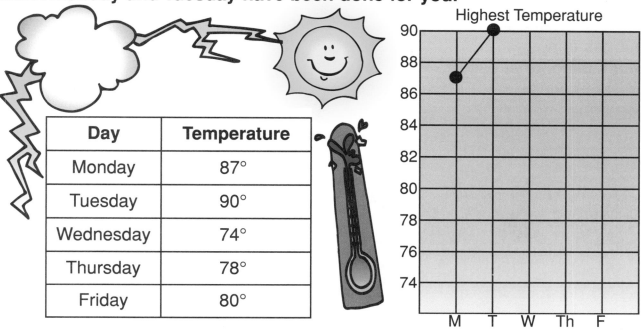

Day	Temperature
Monday	87°
Tuesday	90°
Wednesday	74°
Thursday	78°
Friday	80°

Highest Temperature

Write these sentences in the correct order. Underline the negative word in each sentence. The word that makes the sentence mean "no" or "not" is the negative word.

1. win won't contest I ever art an.

_____

2. involved does want be not He to.

_____

3. today I do have to no work more.

_____

4. nowhere play is us ball There for to.

_____

5. down never let will you God.

_____

6. ridden ever horse Jeremy a hasn't.

_____

Match the definitions below to a word in the Word Box. Find and circle the words in the puzzle. The first one has been done for you.

1. ABC order
2. not a vowel
3. more than one
4. names things
5. mark used for stress
6. part of a word
7. describes nouns

8. used in place of a noun
9. added to the beginning of a base word
10. just one
11. describes verbs
12. not a consonant
13. added to the end of a base word
14. shows action

Word Box

___vowel

___plural

___syllable

_1_alphabetical

___consonant

___prefix

___adjectives

___nouns

___verb

___suffix

___pronoun

___adverbs

___accent

___singular

```
i z x a b u i o m e c f i t x z o c p r u t
u p r t v x o n l k b d f h j l i o m q s t
o o q s u i z a m j a c e g i k o n o u n s
j t s b r c i m s u f f i x b n o s r s t v
f d l v e r b i y q l i g h g a c o d f k l
b c u o x o k r l p u u i o t v e n e h i m
a a f w d z j a l p h a b e t i c a l i p m
p x c e g t l m a x q b c l l b c n j b o t
r u o l n p o k b a d g j t o f t u a i i
y a d v e r b s l c f i l o p r e f i x e l
k d x f g j k l e b e h k i r b f g o e n e
m j z h i o q s r v x y z a o a c c e n t o
l e c m o n p t u l w e a l n w x y z a b c
a c d w e f h j l m n o q r o n o x y z e l
p t e a b e m o e g h i p l u r a l i m o t
s i n g u l a r f j k n i o n e a k l u p x
y v c d e a d e j m v y z i t m l o x z b a
o e b f g k n o q s w f o u l n a d g i m n
e s c h i l p r t y x b c e f h k l o r s t
```

Words to Sound, Read, and Spell

aboard	blindfold	clue	daughter	earliest	fortune	honorable
accept	boathouse	clumsier	dawn	early	forward	hoof
accident	bookcase	clumsiest	debt	earthquake	foster	hospital
account	boring	clumsy	decision	echo	foundation	hotel
ache	borrow	clutch	declare	echoing	fountain	huge
across	boulevard	coach	defense	editor	fourth	human
actress	bowl	coal	definite	education	frequent	humor
additional	breathless	coast	degree	effort	fright	iceberg
advice	bridge	coil	delayed	either	fuel	idea
advise	bridle	collect	delicate	eldest	furious	imagine
affect	brief	collection	delivery	electric	furnace	impatient
afford	brow	comfort	demand	electricity	furniture	import
agency	bruise	comfortable	dentist	enemies	future	important
agree	bucket	comical	describe	enemy	gable	impossible
agriculture	build	commander	desert	engine	gain	increase
alligator	built	committee	deserve	enormous	gallon	index
aloud	bulb	community	despite	enough	garage	indicate
alphabet	burglar	companion	dessert	enthusiasm	geese	innocent
already	bury	company	detective	entrance	generation	inquire
although	bushel	concerns	determination	environment	genuine	insect
among	busiest	conference	determine	envy	germ	inspiring
ancient	business	confess	development	equal	glare	instance
ankle	busy	confirm	diamond	equipment	glaring	instant
announcement	cabin	confusion	dictionary	escape	glorious	instead
answer	cabinet	conjunction	difference	especially	gnaw	institutions
anxious	camera	connect	different	estate	goodness	instructions
appearance	campaign	conquer	difficult	eventually	goose	intention
appreciate	canoes	constant	dignity	evidence	government	interest
approach	captain	contain	dining	exact	governor	interjection
approval	caption	continue	direct	except	graceful	international
approximately	caravan	contribution	director	exchange	graduated	interview
apron	cardboard	conversation	disagree	excitement	graph	introduction
aren't	carefully	convince	disappear	excuse	grateful	investigate
aroma	carpenter	copper	disappoint	exercise	gratitude	island
arranged	carpet	correctly	disaster	exercising	great	jelly
arrival	cartwheel	correspond	discover	existence	grief	jewelry
article	category	cottage	discovery	expect	groan	judgment
assistant	cattle	council	disease	expensive	groceries	juice
association	cedar	country	distance	experience	grocery	junior
assortment	ceiling	county	distant	explanation	grow	justice
assume	center	couple	distrust	explore	grown	kettle
attend	century	coupling	divide	factories	grown-up	kindness
attention	certain	courage	divided	factory	guarantee	kingdom
attic	certainly	cousin	division	familiar	guard	kneel
audience	chalk	cowboy	dizziest	famous	guilty	knit
auditorium	chamber	cozier	dizzy	fancy	habit	knob
author	champion	cozy	doctor	fantastic	hadn't	know
avenue	character	cradle	does	farewell	hail	knowledge
backward	charcoal	crawl	doesn't	farther	handkerchief	known
baggage	cheerful	crazy	dollar	faultless	handsome	label
balcony	chemist	cream	donkeys	favor	happiness	laid
balloon	cherish	creative	doubt	favorite	harness	language
banana	chicken	creature	downstairs	features	haunt	lantern
bathe	chief	crew	downtown	fiction	hawk	laughter
bathroom	chocolate	crossroads	doze	field	he's	lecture
battery	choice	crow	dozen	financial	headquarters	length
battle	choicest	cube	drawer	flapped	health	lettuce
beautiful	choose	cure	drew	flapping	heartily	level
beauty	chose	curious	dried	flattered	heavy	lever
bedtime	chuckled	current	dry	flavor	height	library
beet	circle	curtain	due	flock	histories	lie
behave	circus	custom	dumb	footprint	history	lied
believe	circuses	customer	dump	forecast	hobby	lightning
between	claim	dairy	eagle	forenoon	holiday	limb
bicycle	climate	dangerous	eardrum	forest	homemade	limping
birthday	closet	data	earlier	fortunate	honor	linen

Words to Sound, Read, and Spell

lion	notebook	porch	regular	shine	suspicious	upstairs
liquid	nothing	position	reindeer	shone	sweater	urge
listen	notice	possess	relate	shoulder	sweet	urged
litter	noun	possible	relative	shouldn't	sword	urgent
lonelier	oasis	postscript	relief	show	syllable	useless
loneliest	obey	potato	remarkable	shown	synonym	usual
lonely	object	potatoes	remember	sigh	teach	vacant
loosen	occur	pound	repair	sight	teapot	vain
losing	ocean	poverty	repeat	signal	teaspoon	valuable
loss	offer	powder	replace	silence	teenagers	vanish
lumber	office	practically	replied	simple	teeth	variety
machine	often	practice	reply	singular	telephone	various
machinery	opposite	practicing	report	sleigh	television	vary
mail	orchard	praise	reputation	slept	tennis	vegetable
male	ordinary	precious	rescue	slice	terrible	versus
mankind	original	prefer	resign	slight	terrific	victory
mansion	orphan	prejudice	respect	slim	territory	view
market	ounce	preposition	response	slippery	thaw	violin
marry	outlook	preserve	restore	smooth	there's	vision
marvelous	package	president	retreat	snake	they've	volume
material	paddle	pressure	reward	soar	thief	waist
meadow	pair	price	rise	society	thigh	wait
meal	pajamas	pricing	road	soldier	thirsty	walnut
mean	palm	principal	robin	sorrow	thought	warehouse
meant	pane	private	rocket	south	thousand	warn
measure	partial	privilege	route	soybean	thread	wasn't
measured	particular	probably	rude	spare	throughout	waste
measuring	pass	proceed	ruin	sparrow	thumb	we're
medal	passage	professional	safety	specific	ticket	wealthy
medicine	past	professor	sailor	speech	tied	weary
medium	pasture	promise	saint	spell	tiger	weather
mention	pattern	prompt	salad	spinach	tight	weigh
merchant	pause	prop	salary	splendid	toast	weight
message	peace	prosperous	salute	spoon	toe	welcome
method	peak	protect	satisfaction	sprinkle	together	weren't
midst	pear	prove	satisfy	squeeze	tomato	wheat
mineral	peddle	provide	Saturday	standard	tongue	where's
minus	peek	prune	sawdust	staring	tool	whether
minute	perfect	publicity	scarce	statement	toothbrush	whirl
mirror	performance	puddle	scarcest	station	topic	whistle
miserable	perhaps	pupil	scene	statue	topsoil	whistling
mission	petal	purpose	schedule	steal	total	who's
mistake	piano	purse	scholarship	steel	toward	whom
mixture	picnic	quality	science	stew	tractor	widow
model	picnicking	quart	scissors	sting	traffic	wilderness
modern	picture	quarter	season	stomach	transportation	windshield
moisture	picturing	question	secret	straight	treasure	wise
moment	piece	quiet	secretary	strain	treatment	wolf
month	pigeon	quite	seldom	street	tremendous	woman
moonlight	plain	radish	selfish	stressed	trial	women
most	plane	railroad	senator	stripe	tried	wonderful
motion	planet	rather	senior	stroke	trouble	world
mountain	plantation	reach	sense	struggle	true	worm
museum	platform	real	sensible	stumble	tune	worried
musician	pleasant	reappear	sentencing	success	typewriter	worry
nation	pleasure	rearrange	separate	successes	unfold	worrying
nature	plural	recall	serious	suggest	unhappy	worth
nearby	pocket	recess	serve	suit	uniform	wouldn't
neat	poison	recognition	service	suitcase	union	wreck
necklace	poisonous	recommend	settlement	sunburn	universal	wrestle
necktie	police	record	several	sunshine	university	wrist
needle	policing	recover	severe	superintendent	unknown	you've
neighbor	polish	recovery	shadow	supply	unlike	yourself
nervous	polite	reference	sharpener	supplying	unload	yourselves
newsreel	political	refrigerator	she'll	support	unlock	
northwest	pollution	region	shield	suspect	unlucky	

Answer Pages

Section 1

Page 3

Page 3 (Day 1)

Mixed Skills Practice. Watch the operation signs.

1. 13 - 5 = **8**
2. 17 - 9 = **8**
3. 0 ÷ 3 = **0**
4. 3 x 6 = **18**
5. 6 + 4 = **10**
6. 20 ÷ 4 = **5**
7. 9 ÷ 2 = **11**
8. 1 x 2 = **2**

9. 10 ÷ 2 = **5**
10. 4 x 3 = **12**
11. 13 ÷ 5 = **18**
12. 6 - 0 = **6**
13. 6 x 5 = **30**
14. 15 - 9 = **6**
15. 30 ÷ 6 = **5**
16. 6 ÷ 9 = **15**

17. 27 ÷ 3 = **9**
18. 9 x 7 = **63**
19. 7 + 9 = **16**
20. 25 + 5 = **5**
21. 12 - 4 = **8**
22. 8 + 5 = **13**
23. 13 - 6 = **7**

Find the missing number.

24. 18 ÷ **3** = 6
25. 5 + **1** = 6
26. 10 - **7** = 3
27. 24 ÷ **8** = 3

28. **32** ÷ 4 = 8
29. 3 x **7** = 21
30. **24** ÷ 8 = 3
31. 6 x **3** = 18

32. **6** ÷ 6 = 12
33. 4 x **9** = 36
34. **13** ÷ 6 = 7
35. **0** x 7 = 9

36. 11 - **9** = 2
37. **1** x 8 = 8
38. 10 - **2** = 8
39. 4 + **8** = 12

Write yes before each group of words that make a sentence. Write no if the group is not a sentence. (Remember: A sentence is a group of words that express a complete thought.)

yes 1. Tom carried the canned food.
no 2. Butterflies have beautiful.
no 3. For his tenth birthday.
yes 4. Turtles have hard shells.
yes 5. Everyone enjoyed the trip.
no 6. Have you fastened?
no 7. Wash your hands before.
yes 8. Will you feed the pets?
yes 9. Don't forget to call me.
no 10. Prayed for her.
no 11. We will turn to page.
yes 12. Ants are insects.
yes 13. Do you have hiking boots?
yes 14. Cats are furry.
yes 15. Mark likes to go swimming.
no 16. Our green tent.

3

Page 4 (Day 1)

Food comes in various containers. Write what foods might come in the following containers (or be packaged a certain way). Then list containers of your own.

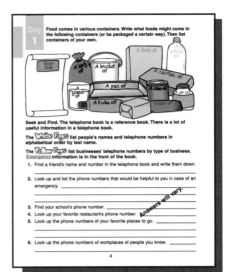

Seek and Find. The telephone book is a reference book. There is a lot of useful information in a telephone book.

The White Pages list people's names and telephone numbers in alphabetical order by last name.

The Yellow Pages list businesses' telephone numbers by type of business. Emergency information is in the front of the book.

1. Find a friend's name and number in the telephone book and write them down. _____
2. Look up and list the phone numbers that would be helpful to you in case of an emergency. _____
3. Find your school's phone number. _____
4. Look up your favorite restaurant's phone number. _____
5. Look up the phone numbers of your favorite places to go. _____
6. Look up the phone numbers of workplaces of people you know. _____

Answers will vary.

4

Page 5 (Day 2)

Add or subtract these 3- or 4-digit numbers.

Helen Keller: The world is moved along...by the aggregate of the tiny pushes of each honest worker.

1. 681 + 145 = **826**
2. 569 - 247 = **322**
3. 3,744 - 1,378 = **2,366**
4. 248 + 48 = **296**
5. 143 + 219 = **362**
6. 2,830 - 519 = **2,311**
7. 9,873 + 828 = **10,701**
8. 5,893 + 3,072 = **8,965**
9. 304 - 172 = **132**
10. 4,918 + 3,928 = **8,846**
11. 6,219 - 4,356 = **1,863**
12. 2,456 + 1,529 = **3,985**
13. 3,375 + 4,518 = **7,893**
14. 428 - 119 = **309**
15. 2,709 + 1,282 = **3,991**
16. 7,645 - 564 = **7,081**
17. 1,680 - 354 = **1,326**
18. 6,142 - 2,525 = **3,617**

Add the correct word—their or there. Remember: their means "they own" or "have," and there means "in or at the place," or it can begin a sentence.

1. **There** must be something wrong with that cow.
2. The Hills were training **their** horse to jump.
3. We are going to **their** farm tomorrow.
4. Please put the boxes over **there**.
5. **There** will be sixteen people at the party.
6. Will you please sit here, not **there**?
7. **Their** barn burned down yesterday.
8. They will put **their** animals in Mr. Jack's barn tonight.

Write four sentences about your church. Use their in two of them and there in the other two.

9. 10. 11. 12.

Sentences will vary.

5

Page 6 (Day 2)

Suffixes. A suffix is a syllable added to the end of a base word. Add the suffix in the middle of the suffix wheel to the end of the base word. Write the new word. Remember: You may need to double the final consonant or change a y to an i when adding a suffix.

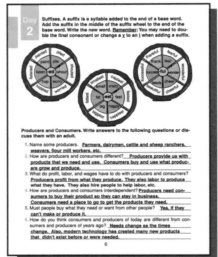

Producers and Consumers. Write answers to the following questions or discuss them with an adult.

1. Name some producers. **Farmers, dairymen, cattle and sheep ranchers, weavers, flour mill workers, etc.**
2. How are producers and consumers different? **Producers provide us with products that we need and use. Consumers buy and use what producers grow and produce.**
3. What do profit, labor, and wages have to do with producers and consumers? **Producers profit from what they produce. They also labor to produce what they have. They also hire people to help labor, etc.**
4. How are producers and consumers interdependent? **Producers need consumers to buy their product so they can stay in business. Consumers need a place to go to get the products they need.**
5. Must people buy what they need or want from other people? **Yes, if they can't make or produce it.**
6. How do you think consumers and producers of years ago are different from consumers and producers of today? **Needs change as the times change. Also, modern technology has created many new products that didn't exist before or were needed.**

6

Page 7 (Day 3)

Understanding Thousands. Write each number in standard form. The first one has been done for you.

1. 8 thousands, 3 tens, 9 ones = **8,039**
2. 6,000 + 300 + 10 + 2 = **6,312**
3. 3 thousands, 8 hundreds, 4 tens, 1 one = **3,841**
4. 5,000 + 700 + 3 = **5,703**
5. 7 thousands, 1 hundred, 7 ones = **7,107**
6. 9,000 + 900 + 90 + 9 = **9,999**
7. 2 thousands, 9 hundreds, 6 tens, 2 ones = **2,962**
8. 1,000 + 8 = **1,008**
9. 1 thousand, 7 tens, 5 ones = **1,075**
10. 2,000 + 900 + 80 + 9 = **2,989**
11. 6 thousands, 9 hundreds, 9 tens, 6 ones = **6,996**
12. 1,000 + 400 + 10 = **1,410**
13. 0 thousands, 4 hundreds, 7 tens = **470**
14. 7,000 + 900 + 5 = **7,905**
15. 4 thousands, 5 tens = **4,050**
16. 3,000 + 10 + 5 = **3,015**

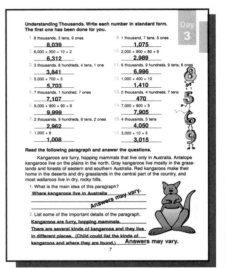

Read the following paragraph and answer the questions.

Kangaroos are furry, hopping mammals that live only in Australia. Antelope kangaroos live on the plains in the north. Gray kangaroos live mostly in the grasslands and forests of eastern and southern Australia. Red kangaroos make their home in the deserts and dry grasslands in the central part of the country, and most wallaroos live in dry, rocky hills.

1. What is the main idea of this paragraph? **Where kangaroos live in Australia.** *Answers may vary.*
2. List some of the important details of the paragraph. **Kangaroos are furry, hopping mammals. There are several kinds of kangaroos and they live in different places.** (Child could list the kinds of kangaroos and where they are found.) *Answers may vary.*

7

Page 8 (Day 3)

Products. What products might we get from the seven major regions of our country? See if you can put the correct region next to the correct products.

• Great Lakes • Mountain • Southwest • Northeast
• Plains • Pacific • Southeast

Southeast 1. The main crops are sugarcane, oranges, soybeans, rice, peanuts, and tobacco. The main minerals are oil, iron ore, limestone, and coal. Hickory, oak, maple, and lots of other trees are used for furniture, paper, and other products.

Northeast 2. Lots of different kinds of fish and shellfish are found here: cod, butterfish, clams, lobsters, squid, sea bass, flounder, sole, and swordfish. Farm products include milk, cheese, eggs, fruits, vegetables, chickens, turkeys, tomatoes, blueberries, cranberries, maple syrup, and grapes. This region also produces lots of coal.

Plains 3. Record amounts of corn, soybeans, and oats are found here. Other crops include fruits and vegetables. This area is rich in minerals, iron ore, and coal. This area is also rich in dairy products. This is called the "Corn Belt" of the United States.

Great Lakes 4. Corn and wheat grow well here. A lot of farming, ranching, and mining is done here. This area manufactures a lot of hot dogs, flour, and breakfast cereals.

Southwest 5. The largest crop in this area is cotton. Other crops are oranges, grapefruit, rice, and wheat. They raise a lot of cattle and sheep here. Silver and copper are found in this region. Fuels are also plentiful, such as coal, natural gas, uranium, and oil.

Pacific 6. A wide variety of products come from here because of the two very different climate areas. Products include oil, king crab, salmon, and timber, as well as pineapple, macadamia nuts, fruits, nuts, berries, and vegetables. This area also produces petroleum and natural gas. It has the top agricultural state in the nation, as well as the top commercial fishing region.

Mountain 7. Some of the major minerals found in this region are gold, lead, silver, copper, and zinc. There is also lots of natural gas, coal, and oil to be found. Wheat, peas, beans, sugar beets, and potatoes are grown here. Ranching includes beef cattle, sheep, and dairy cows.

8

Page 9 (Day 4)

Estimating Sums and Differences. When estimating numbers, round them off, then add or subtract. Remember: Answers are not exact.

EXAMPLE: 420 + 384 = ___. 420 is close to 400, and 384 is close to 400, so your answer would be 800 when estimating. Try estimating these problems!

1. 88 + 19 = 90 + 20 = **110**
2. 81 + 75 = 80 + 80 = **160**
3. 93 - 85 = 90 - 90 = **0**
4. 98 - 39 = 100 - 110 = **100**
5. 93 - 39 = 90 - 40 = **50**
6. 891 - 551 = 900 - 600 = **300**
7. 57 - 39 = 60 - 40 = **20**
8. 24 + 35 = 20 + 40 = **60**
9. 209 + 179 = 200 + 200 = **400**
10. 56 + 33 = 60 - 30 = **30**
11. 56 - 33 = 60 - 30 = **30**
12. 288 + 398 = 300 + 400 = **700**
13. 78 - 18 = 80 - 20 = **60**
14. 75 - 42 = 80 - 40 = **40**
15. 540 + 317 = 300 + 300 = **800**
16. 66 + 12 = 70 + 10 = **80**
17. 30 + 71 = 30 + 70 = **100**
18. 610 - 273 = 600 - 300 = **300**
19. 63 + 93 = 60 + 90 = **150**
20. 91 + 65 = 90 + 70 = **160**
21. 247 - 210 = 200 - 200 = **0**

Write the five steps to the writing or composition process. (See page 59 if you need help.) Then write a short story of your own. Use all five steps. You will need additional paper.

1. prewriting or choose a topic
2. Write a first draft.
3. Revise-add to, change
4. Proofread-make corrections
5. Publish or make final copy

Story: _____ *Story will vary.*

9

Page 10 (Day 4)

Prefixes. Prefixes are syllables added to the beginning of a base word. Add a prefix to these base words. The first one has been done for you.

1. Will you **un** lock the door?
2. Can you **re** call what he said?
3. The brownies seemed to **dis** appear after the boys saw them.
4. Janet will **un** fold the napkins.
5. Do you **dis** agree with what I said?
6. Mother is going to **re** arrange the front room.
7. The picture was the shape of a **tri** angle.
8. Everyone needs to come **a** board again.
9. Erin and Eli will wear **uni** forms to the game.
10. You can count on me to **re** pay you.
11. Look out for the **on** coming traffic!
12. The Damons have six **tele** phones in their house.
13. There is a big **dis** count on the cost of this table.
14. That was a very **un** wise thing to do.

Local, State, and Federal Government Activity. Use a telephone directory to look up listings under local, state, and federal government. Record some at each level.

Local	Federal	State
	Answers will vary.	

10

Page 11

Day 5

Number Families. You can practice basic math facts by using "families of facts."

7 + 2 = 9 2 + 7 = 9 9 - 2 = 7 9 - 7 = 2
3 x 6 = 18 6 x 3 = 18 18 ÷ 3 = 6 18 ÷ 6 = 3

Complete the number families below.

1. 9, 7, 16	2. 3, 9, 27	3. 4, 8, 32	4. 8, 5, 40
9 + 7 = 16	3 x 9 = 27	4 x 8 = 32	8 x 5 = 40
7 + 9 = 16	9 x 3 = 27	8 x 4 = 32	5 x 8 = 40
16 - 9 = 7	27 ÷ 3 = 9	32 ÷ 4 = 8	40 ÷ 8 = 5
16 - 7 = 9	27 ÷ 9 = 3	32 ÷ 8 = 4	40 ÷ 5 = 8
5. 3, 8, 11	6. 3, 4, 12	7. 12, 11, 23	8. 612, 208, 820
3 + 8 = 11	3 x 4 = 12	12 + 11 = 23	612 + 208 = 820
8 + 3 = 11	4 x 3 = 12	11 + 12 = 23	208 + 612 = 820
11 - 3 = 8	12 ÷ 3 = 4	23 - 11 = 12	820 - 612 = 208
11 - 8 = 3	12 ÷ 4 = 3	23 - 12 = 11	820 - 208 = 612

Nouns are words that name people, places, or things.
Common nouns name any person, place, or thing.
Proper nouns name a particular person, place, or thing.
Draw a circle around the common nouns and underline the proper nouns in the following sentences. The first one has been done for you.

1. There are many (missionaries) in Africa.
2. Christopher Columbus was an (explorer).
3. Antarctica is a (continent).
4. The (ships) crossed the Atlantic Ocean.
5. We paddled the (canoe) down the Red River.
6. (Astronauts) explore (space) for the United States.
7. San Francisco is the (city) by the (bay).
8. Julie and Ashley visited their (aunt) in Boston.
9. Mt. Smart is a small (mountain) in Idaho.
10. Thursday is Andrew's (birthday).
11. What (state) does Mike live in?
12. Are Hilary and her (brother) going to the (circus)?
13. Brian went to the (library) to get some (books).

11

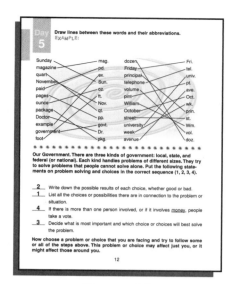

Page 12

Day 5

Draw lines between these words and their abbreviations.
EXAMPLE:

Sunday	mag.	dozen	Fri.
magazine	pd.	Friday	tel.
quart	ex.	principal	univ.
November	Sun.	telephone	pt.
paid	oz.	volume	ave.
pages	ft.	pint	Oct.
ounce	Nov.	William	wk.
package	qt.	October	prin.
Doctor	pp.	street	st.
example	govt.	university	Wm.
government	Dr.	week	vol.
foot	pkg.	avenue	doz.

Our Government. There are three kinds of government: local, state, and federal (or national). Each kind handles problems of different sizes. They try to solve problems that people cannot solve alone. Put the following statements on problem solving and choices in the correct sequence (1, 2, 3, 4).

__2__ Write down the possible results of each choice, whether good or bad.
__1__ List all the choices or possibilities there are in connection to the problem or situation.
__4__ If there is more than one person involved, or if it involves money, people take a vote.
__3__ Decide what is most important and which choice or choices will best solve the problem.

Now choose a problem or choice that you are facing and try to follow some or all of the steps above. This problem or choice may affect just you, or it might affect those around you.

12

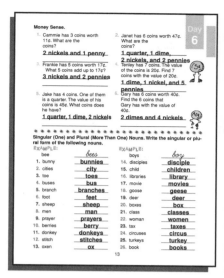

Page 13

Day 6

Money Sense.

1. Cammie has 3 coins worth 11¢. What are the coins? **2 nickels and 1 penny**
2. Janet has 6 coins worth 47¢. What are the coins? **1 quarter, 1 dime, 2 nickels, and 2 pennies**
3. Frankie has 5 coins worth 17¢. What 5 coins add up to 17¢? **3 nickels and 2 pennies**
4. Tenley has 7 coins. The value of the coins is 20¢. Find 7 coins with the value of 20¢. **1 dime, 1 nickel, and 5 pennies**
5. Jake has 4 coins. One of them is a quarter. The value of his coins is 45¢. What coins does he have? **1 quarter, 1 dime, 2 nickels**
6. Gary has 6 coins worth 40¢. Find the 6 coins that Gary has with the value of 40¢. **2 dimes and 4 nickels**

Singular (One) and Plural (More Than One) Nouns. Write the singular or plural form of the following nouns.

EXAMPLE: bee	*bees*	EXAMPLE: boys	*boy*
1. bunny	**bunnies**	14. disciples	**disciple**
2. cities	**city**	15. child	**children**
3. toe	**toes**	16. libraries	**library**
4. buses	**bus**	17. movie	**movies**
5. branch	**branches**	18. goose	**geese**
6. foot	**feet**	19. deer	**deer**
7. sheep	**sheep**	20. boxes	**box**
8. men	**man**	21. class	**classes**
9. prayer	**prayers**	22. woman	**women**
10. berries	**berry**	23. tax	**taxes**
11. donkey	**donkeys**	24. circuses	**circus**
12. stitch	**stitches**	25. turkeys	**turkey**
13. oxen	**ox**	26. book	**books**

13

Page 14

Day 6

Which word referent should be used in place of the word or words in parentheses? Write it in the blank. He, she, you, it, they, him, her, them, then, here, us, and there are all word referents.

Barbara and Denise were best friends. (Barbara and Denise) **They** had decided to go on a trip together this summer. With maps and brochures scattered all over Barbara's floor, (Barbara and Denise) **they** started looking for a place to go. One brochure described an interesting place. (The brochure) **It** was about Yellowstone Park. "Let's go (Yellowstone) **there**!" cried Denise. "(Yellowstone) **It** would be a fun place to go. I think we should ask my brother to go with us," said Barbara. "(My brother) **He** could do a lot of the driving for (Barbara and Denise) **us**."

Tom's car was packed and ready to go the next morning. (The car) **It** was a new 4x4 Ranger. (Barbara, Denise, and Tom) **They** would have taken Barbara's car, but (Barbara's) **her** car had a flat tire.

After driving for two days, the travelers got to Yellowstone Park. Tom shouted, "At last we are (at Yellowstone) **here**!" (Tom) **He** was tired of driving. (The trip) **It** turned out to be a fun trip for (Denise, Barbara, and Tom) **them**.

Points of Interest. What makes the state, town, or country that you live in an interesting place? Write an advertisement to get people to visit or even live in your state, town, or country. What are the points of interest? What makes it special and different from other places?

Answers will vary.

14

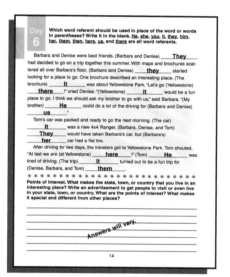

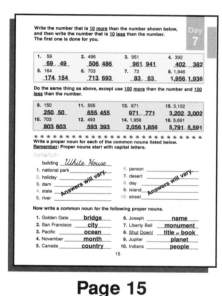

Page 15

Day 7

Write the number that is 10 more than the number shown below, and then write the number that is 10 less than the number. The first one is done for you.

1. 59: 69, 49	2. 496: 506, 486	3. 951: 961, 941	4. 392: 402, 382
5. 164: 174, 154	6. 703: 713, 693	7. 73: 83, 63	8. 1,946: 1,956, 1,936

Do the same thing as above, except use 100 more than the number and 100 less than the number.

9. 150: 250, 50	11. 555: 655, 455	13. 871: 971, 771	15. 3,102: 3,202, 3,002
10. 703: 803, 603	12. 493: 593, 393	14. 1,956: 2,056, 1,856	16. 5,691: 5,791, 5,591

Write a proper noun for each of the common nouns listed below.
Remember: Proper nouns start with capital letters.

EXAMPLE: building *White House*

1. national park
2. holiday
3. dam
4. state
5. river
6. person
7. desert
8. day
9. island
10. street

Answers will vary. Answers will vary.

Now write a common noun for the following proper nouns.

1. Golden Gate **bridge**
2. San Francisco **city**
3. Pacific **ocean**
4. November **month**
5. Canada **country**
6. Joseph **name**
7. Liberty Bell **monument**
8. Shut Down! **title or book**
9. Jupiter **planet**
10. Indians **people**

15

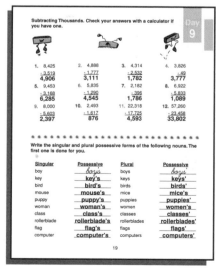

Page 16

Day 7

Father's Day. Write about fathers, then draw a picture. Fathers should always... Father should never... If I were a father, I would want to always...

Stories will vary.

Draw your picture here!

16

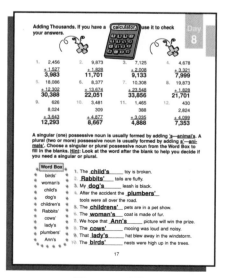

Page 17

Day 8

Adding Thousands. If you have a (calculator), use it to check your answers.

1. 2,456 + 1,527 = **3,983**	2. 9,873 + 1,828 = **11,701**	3. 7,125 + 2,008 = **9,133**	4. 4,678 + 3,321 = **7,999**
5. 18,086 + 12,302 = **30,388**	6. 8,377 + 13,674 = **22,051**	7. 10,308 + 23,548 = **33,856**	8. 19,873 + 1,828 = **21,701**
9. 626 + 8,024 + 3,643 = **12,293**	10. 3,481 + 309 + 4,877 = **8,667**	11. 1,465 + 388 + 3,035 = **4,888**	12. 430 + 2,824 + 4,099 = **7,353**

A singular (one) possessive noun is usually formed by adding 's—animal's. A plural (two or more) possessive noun is usually formed by adding s'—animals'. Choose a singular or plural possessive noun from the Word Box to fill in the blanks. Hint: Look at the word after the blank to help you decide if you need a singular or plural.

Word Box: birds', woman's, child's, dog's, children's, Rabbits', cows', lady's, plumbers', Ann's

1. The **child's** toy is broken.
2. **Rabbits'** tails are fluffy.
3. My **dog's** leash is black.
4. After the accident the **plumbers'** tools were all over the road.
5. The **childrens'** pets are in a pet show.
6. The **woman's** coat is made of fur.
7. We hope that **Ann's** picture will win the prize.
8. The **cows'** mooing was loud and noisy.
9. That **lady's** hat blew away in the windstorm.
10. The **birds'** nests were high up in the trees.

17

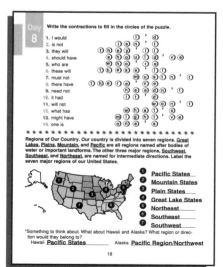

Page 18

Day 8

Write the contractions to fill in the circles of the puzzle.

1. I would — I'd
2. is not — isn't
3. they will — they'll
4. should have — should've
5. who are — who're
6. these will — these'll
7. must not — mustn't
8. there have — there've
9. need not — needn't
10. it had — it'd
11. will not — won't
12. what has — what's
13. might have — might've
14. one is — one's

Regions of Our Country. Our country is divided into seven regions. Great Lakes, Plains, Mountain, and Pacific are all regions named after bodies of water or important landforms. The other three major regions, Southwest, Southeast, and Northeast, are named for intermediate directions. Label the seven major regions of our United States.

1. **Pacific States**
2. **Mountain States**
3. **Plain States**
4. **Great Lake States**
5. **Northeast**
6. **Southeast**
7. **Southwest**

*Something to think about. What about Hawaii and Alaska? What region or direction would they belong to?
Hawaii **Pacific States** Alaska **Pacific Region/Northwest**

18

Page 19

Day 9

Subtracting Thousands. Check your answers with a calculator if you have one.

1. 8,425 - 3,519 = **4,906**	2. 4,888 - 1,777 = **3,111**	3. 4,314 - 2,532 = **1,782**	4. 3,826 - 49 = **3,777**
5. 9,453 - 3,168 = **6,285**	6. 5,835 - 1,290 = **4,545**	7. 2,182 - 396 = **1,786**	8. 6,922 - 5,833 = **1,089**
9. 8,000 - 5,603 = **2,397**	10. 2,493 - 1,617 = **876**	11. 22,318 - 17,725 = **4,593**	12. 57,260 - 23,458 = **33,802**

Write the singular and plural possessive forms of the following nouns. The first one is done for you.

Singular	Possessive	Plural	Possessive
boy	*boy's*	boys	*boys'*
key	**key's**	keys	**keys'**
bird	**bird's**	birds	**birds'**
mouse	**mouse's**	mice	**mice's**
puppy	**puppy's**	puppies	**puppies'**
woman	**woman's**	women	**women's**
class	**class's**	classes	**classes'**
rollerblade	**rollerblade's**	rollerblades	**rollerblades'**
flag	**flag's**	flags	**flags'**
computer	**computer's**	computers	**computers'**

19

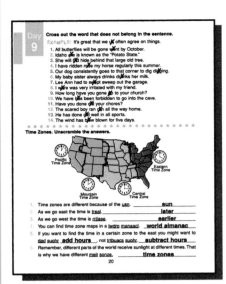

Day 9

Cross out the word that does not belong in the sentence.

EXAMPLE: It's great that we *often* agree on things.

1. All butterflies will be gone *went* by October.
2. Idaho *site* is known as the "Potato State."
3. She will *did* hide behind that large old tree.
4. I have ridden *rode* my horse regularly this summer.
5. Our dog consistently goes to that corner to dig *digging* there.
6. My baby sister always drinks *drinks* her milk.
7. Lee Ann had to *rejot* sweep out the garage.
8. I *were* was very irritated with my friend.
9. How long have you gone *go* to your church?
10. We have *has* been forbidden to go into the cave.
11. Have you done *did* your chores?
12. The scared boy ran *run* all the way home.
13. He has done *did* well in all sports.
14. The wind has *blew* blown for five days.

Time Zones. Unscramble the answers.

1. Time zones are different because of the *usn*. **sun**
2. As we go east the time is *treal*. **later**
3. As we go west the time is *rilaee*. **earlier**
4. You can find time zone maps in a *hydro manaacl*. **world almanac**
5. If you want to find the time in a certain zone to the east you might want to *dad suohr* **add hours**, not *trbuaca suohr*. **subtract hours**
6. Remember, different parts of the world receive sunlight at different times. That is why we have different *meil sonze*. **time zones**

20

Page 21

Day 10

Multiplication. Find each product.

EXAMPLE:

1. 9 x 2 = 18
2. 8 x 4 = **32**
3. 5 x 6 = **30**
4. 7 x 3 = **21**
5. 4 x 6 = **24**
6. 9 x 5 = **45**
7. 8 x 6 = **48**
8. 5 x 7 = **35**
9. 3 x 9 = **27**
10. 7 x 6 = **42**
11. 1 x 9 = **9**

12. 4 x 7 = **28**
13. 8 x 3 = **24**
14. 3 x 3 = **9**
15. 3 x 6 = **18**
16. 6 x 9 = **54**
17. 9 x 5 = **45**
18. 9 x 4 = **36**
19. 7 x 7 = **49**
20. 7 x 8 = **56**
21. 7 x 9 = **63**
22. 9 x 9 = **81**

23. 8 x 5 = **40**
24. 3 x 4 = **12**
25. 5 x 5 = **25**
26. 8 x 7 = **56**
27. 7 x 3 = **21**
28. 8 x 8 = **64**
29. 9 x11 = **99**
30. 9 x10 = **90**
31. 9 x 7 = **63**
32. 8 x 9 = **72**

Main Verbs and Helping Verbs. Helping verbs help the main verb. The main verb shows action. Underline the main verb. Circle the helping verbs.

1. It *has been* raining for five days.
2. Jack *had* finished his lessons before 10:00.
3. I *have* enjoyed the children this month.
4. We *were* cleaning the house for our friend.
5. The babies *have been* sleeping for two hours.
6. Two rafts *were* floating down the river.

Fill in the blank with a helping verb.

7. David **was** diving into the pond.
8. The pool **hadn't been** used all summer.
9. I **had been** waiting for them to fix it.
10. They **haven't been** working on it for three weeks.
11. It **hasn't been** fun without the pool.
12. Seven sheep **were** running loose in the street.

21

Page 22

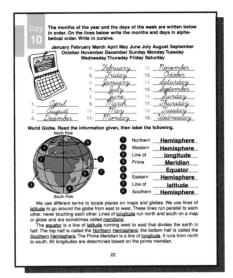

Day 10

The months of the year and the days of the week are written below in order. On the lines below write the months and days in alphabetical order. Write in cursive.

January February March April May June July August September October November December Sunday Monday Tuesday Wednesday Thursday Friday Saturday

1. *April*
2. *August*
3. *December*
4. *February*
5. *Friday*
6. *January*
7. *July*
8. *June*
9. *March*
10. *May*
11. *Monday*
12. *November*
13. *October*
14. *Saturday*
15. *September*
16. *Sunday*
17. *Thursday*
18. *Tuesday*
19. *Wednesday*

World Globe. Read the information given, then label the following.

1. Northern **Hemisphere**
2. Western **Hemisphere**
3. Line of **longitude**
4. Prime **Meridian**
5. **Equator**
6. Eastern **Hemisphere**
7. Line of **latitude**
8. Southern **Hemisphere**

We use different terms to locate places on maps and globes. We use lines of latitude to go around the globe from east to west. These lines run parallel to each other, never touching each other. Lines of longitude run north and south on a map or globe and are sometimes called meridians.

The equator is a line of latitude running west to east that divides the earth in half. The top half is called the Northern Hemisphere; the bottom half is called the Southern Hemisphere. The Prime Meridian is a line of longitude. It runs from north to south. All longitudes are determined based on the prime meridian.

22

Page 23   Page 24   Page 25

Day 11

Adding or Subtracting Thousands. Check your answers using a calculator if you have one.

1. 7,458 − 3,762 = **3,696**
2. 8,562 + 2,163 = **10,725**
3. 5,585 − 2,609 = **2,976**
4. 6,052 − 5,381 = **671**
5. 7,871 + 1,695 = **9,566**

6. 36,814 − 7,523 = **29,291**
7. 53,397 + 39,288 = **92,685**
8. 19,506 + 34,947 = **54,453**
9. 18,103 − 9,079 = **9,024**
10. 43,470 − 3,746 = **39,724**

11. 3,245 + 5,029 + 6,981 = **15,255**
12. 9,421 + 8,389 + 4,506 = **22,316**
13. 3,340 + 7,189 + 4,482 = **15,011**
14. 46,306 + 18,782 + 3,115 = **68,203**
15. 36,814 + 17,288 + 29,397 = **83,499**

Present tense verbs happen now. Past tense verbs have already happened. Write the past or present tense for these verbs.

EXAMPLE: stay—present tense; stayed—past tense.

Present	Past	Present	Past
1. hop	**hopped**	6. **thank**	thanked
2. skate	**skated**	7. **call**	called
3. love	**loved**	8. **sprain**	sprained
4. play	**played**	9. **wrap**	wrapped
5. work	**worked**	10. **hug**	hugged

Past Tense with a Helper. Write the past tense.

EXAMPLE:

Present Tense	Past Tense with Helping Verb
1. walk	has, have, had *walked*
2. jog	has, have, had **jogged**
3. pray	has, have, had **prayed**
4. empty	has, have, had **emptied**
5. chase	has, have, had **chased**

23

Page 24

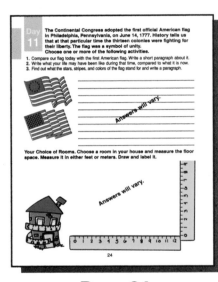

Day 11

The Continental Congress adopted the first official American flag in Philadelphia, Pennsylvania, on June 14, 1777. History tells us that at that particular time the thirteen colonies were fighting for their liberty. The flag was a symbol of unity. Choose one or more of the following activities.

1. Compare our flag today with the first American flag. Write a short paragraph about it.
2. Write what your life may have been like during that time, compared to what it is now.
3. Find out what the stars, stripes, and colors of the flag stand for and write a paragraph.

Answers will vary.

Your Choice of Rooms. Choose a room in your house and measure the floor space. Measure it in either feet or meters. Draw and label it.

Answers will vary.

24

Page 25

Day 12

Division. Find each quotient.

1. 20 ÷ 4 = **5**
2. 28 ÷ 4 = **7**
3. 14 ÷ 7 = **2**
4. 42 ÷ 6 = **7**
5. 6 ÷ 6 = **0**
6. 30 ÷ 5 = **6**
7. 32 ÷ 4 = **8**
8. 25 ÷ 5 = **5**
9. 81 ÷ 9 = **9**
10. 49 ÷ 7 = **7**
11. 18 ÷ 6 = **3**
12. 63 ÷ 7 = **9**
13. 40 ÷ 5 = **8**
14. 36 ÷ 9 = **4**
15. 72 ÷ 9 = **8**
16. 54 ÷ 6 = **9**
17. 48 ÷ 6 = **8**
18. 32 ÷ 8 = **4**
19. 45 ÷ 9 = **5**
20. 36 ÷ 6 = **6**
21. 54 ÷ 9 = **6**
22. 48 ÷ 8 = **6**
23. 63 ÷ 7 = **9**
24. 99 ÷ 9 = **11**

Fill in the blanks with the past tense verb. Hint: You will have to change the spelling. The first one is done for you.

Past Tense

1. Bells ring. Bells *rang*
2. We eat. We **ate**
3. I wear it. I **wore** it.
4. You make some. You **made** some.
5. They sing. They **sang**
6. I throw. I **threw**
7. I say. I **said**
8. They take. They **took**

Fill in the blank with the past tense of the verb.

9. Sam **knew** he wanted to stay in touch with Kit. (know)
10. Katie **wrote** a letter to Ron. (write)
11. He **brought** his friend with him. (bring)
12. The pastor **began** the sermon. (begin)
13. That little girl **broke** her doll again. (break)
14. I **drove** her new car to the play. (drive)

25

Page 26   Page 27   Page 28

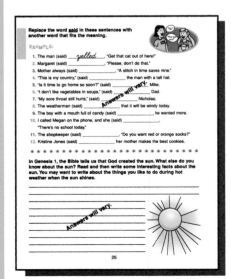

Replace the word *said* in these sentences with another word that fits the meaning.

EXAMPLE:

1. The man (said) *yelled*, "Get that cat out of here!"
2. Margaret (said) _____, "Please, don't do that."
3. Mother always (said) _____, "A stitch in time saves nine."
4. "This is my country," (said) _____ the man with a tall hat.
5. "Is it time to go home so soon?" (said) _____ Mike.
6. "I don't like vegetables in soups." (said) _____ Dad.
7. "My sore throat still hurts." (said) _____ Nicholas.
8. The weatherman (said) _____ that it will be windy today.
9. The boy with a mouth full of candy (said) _____ he wanted more.
10. I called Megan on the phone, and she (said) _____ "There's no school today."
11. The shopkeeper (said) _____, "Do you want red or orange socks?"
12. Kristine Jones (said) _____ her mother makes the best cookies.

Answers will vary.

In Genesis 1, the Bible tells us that God created the sun. What else do you know about the sun? Read and then write some interesting facts about the sun. You may want to write about the things you like to do during hot weather when the sun shines.

Answers will vary.

26

Page 27

Day 13

Multiplication with Three Factors. Find the product of the three factors.

EXAMPLE: 6 x 1 x 3 = 6 x 1 = 6 x 3 = 18

1. 2 x 4 x 2 = **16**
2. 3 x 3 x 5 = **45**
3. 4 x 2 x 2 = **16**
4. 2 x 5 x 1 = **10**
5. 4 x 2 x 4 = **32**
6. 2 x 3 x 7 = **42**
7. 0 x 9 x 9 = **0**
8. 3 x 2 x 3 = **18**
9. 3 x 3 x 3 = **27**
10. 5 x 2 x 2 = **20**
11. 4 x 2 x 5 = **40**
12. 2 x 3 x 6 = **36**
13. 1 x 2 x 3 = **6**
14. 3 x 3 x 0 = **0**
15. 3 x 5 x 0 = **0**
16. 1 x 3 x 5 = **15**
17. 2 x 3 x 4 = **24**
18. 2 x 2 x 3 = **12**
19. 4 x 3 x 2 = **24**
20. 8 x 1 x 8 = **64**
21. 3 x 3 x 8 = **72**
22. 3 x 5 x 1 = **15**
23. 6 x 3 x 1 = **18**
24. 4 x 1 x 3 = **12**

Write four sentences using the word *are*. Write four sentences using the word *our*. The first two are done for you.

1. *Our* house is almost finished.
2. When *are* you going to live in it?
3. _____
4. _____
5. _____
6. _____
7. _____
8. _____

Sentences will vary.

Now write two sentences using *it's* and *its*. Remember: *It's* is a contraction of *it is*, and *its* is a possessive pronoun.

1. _____
2. _____
3. _____
4. _____

Sentences will vary.

27

Page 28

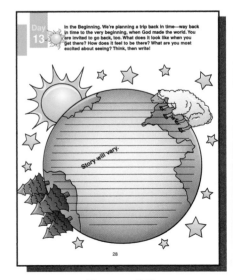

Day 13

In the Beginning. We're planning a trip back in time—way back in time to the very beginning, when God made the world. How are you invited to go back, too. What does it look like when you get there? How does it feel to be there? What are you most excited about seeing? Think, then write!

Story will vary.

28

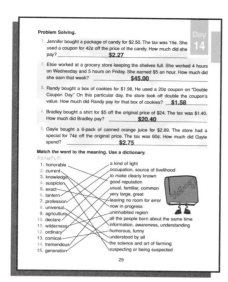

Page 29

Problem Solving.

1. Jennifer bought a package of candy for $2.50. The tax was 19¢. She used a coupon for 42¢ off the price of the candy. How much did she pay? **$2.27**
2. Elsie worked at a grocery store keeping the shelves full. She worked 4 hours on Wednesday and 5 hours on Friday. She earned $5 an hour. How much did she earn that week? **$45.00**
3. Randy bought a box of cookies for $1.98. He used a 20¢ coupon on "Double Coupon Day." On this particular day, the store took off double the coupon's value. How much did Randy pay for that box of cookies? **$1.58**
4. Bradley bought a shirt for $5 off the original price of $24. The tax was $1.40. How much did Bradley pay? **$20.40**
5. Gayle bought a 6-pack of canned orange juice for $2.89. The store had a special for 74¢ off the original price. The tax was 60¢. How much did Gayle spend? **$2.75**

Match the word to the meaning. Use a dictionary.

1. honorable — good reputation
2. current — now in progress
3. knowledge — information, awareness, understanding
4. suspicion — suspecting or being suspected
5. exact — leaving no room for error
6. lantern — a kind of light
7. profession — occupation, source of livelihood
8. universal — understood by all
9. agriculture — the science and art of farming
10. declare — to make clearly known
11. wilderness — uninhabited region
12. ordinary — usual, familiar, common
13. comical — humorous, funny
14. tremendous — very large, great
15. generation — all the people born about the same time

29

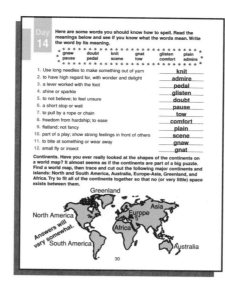

Page 30

Here are some words you should know how to spell. Read the meanings below and see if you know what the words mean. Write the word by its meaning.

gnaw doubt knit gnat glisten plain
pause pedal scene tow comfort admire

1. Use long needles to make something out of yarn — **knit**
2. to have high regard for, with wonder and delight — **admire**
3. a lever worked with the foot — **pedal**
4. shine or sparkle — **glisten**
5. to not believe; to feel unsure — **doubt**
6. a short stop or wait — **pause**
7. to pull by a rope or chain — **tow**
8. freedom from hardship; to ease — **comfort**
9. flatland; not fancy — **plain**
10. part of a play; show strong feelings in front of others — **scene**
11. to bite at something or wear away — **gnaw**
12. small fly or insect — **gnat**

Continents. Have you ever really looked at the shapes of the continents on a world map? It almost seems as if the continents are part of a big puzzle. Find a world map, then trace and cut out the following major continents and islands: North and South America, Australia, Europe-Asia, Greenland, and Africa. Try to fit all of the continents together so that no (or very little) space exists between them.

Answers will vary somewhat.

Greenland, North America, South America, Europe, Asia, Africa, Australia

30

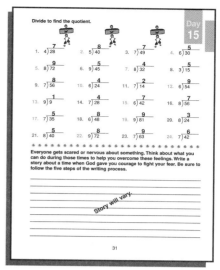

Page 31

Divide to find the quotient.

1. 4)28 = 7
2. 5)40 = 8
3. 7)49 = 7
4. 6)30 = 5
5. 8)72 = 9
6. 9)45 = 5
7. 8)32 = 4
8. 3)15 = 5
9. 7)56 = 8
10. 6)24 = 4
11. 7)14 = 2
12. 6)54 = 9
13. 9)9 = 1
14. 7)28 = 4
15. 6)42 = 7
16. 8)56 = 7
17. 3)15 = 5
18. 6)48 = 8
19. 9)81 = 9
20. 8)24 = 3
21. 5)40 = 8
22. 9)72 = 8
23. 7)63 = 9
24. 7)42 = 6

Everyone gets scared or nervous about something. Think about what you can do during those times to help you overcome these feelings. Write a story about a time when God gave you courage to fight your fear. Be sure to follow the five steps of the writing process.

Story will vary.

31

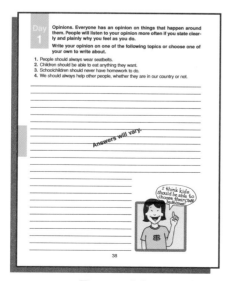

Page 32

Below are the days of the week and the months of the year spelled with dictionary symbols. Write the words to the side. Don't forget capital letters. The first one is done for you.

1. /ā′prel/ — April
2. /jan′ūre′ē/ — January
3. /mun′dā/ — Monday
4. /sep tem′bәr/ — September
5. /dē sem′bәr/ — December
6. /sat′әr dā/ — Saturday
7. /mā/ — May
8. /feb′rūer′ē/ — February
9. /tūz′dā/ — Tuesday
10. /frī′dā/ — Friday
11. /märch/ — March
12. /wenz′dā/ — Wednesday
13. /jūn/ — June
14. /sun′dā/ — Sunday
15. /nō vem′bәr/ — November
16. /o′gest/ — August
17. /thәrz′dā/ — Thursday
18. /ok tō bәr/ — October
19. /jūlī′/ — July

Rocks. Rocks are found almost everywhere. There is much to see and learn about rocks. Geologists are scientists who study rocks. All rocks are made up of one or more minerals. Scientists have discovered over 2,000 minerals. Rocks are changed by water, plants, and other forces of nature. Below are words you need to know when talking about rocks. Look up each word in the dictionary and write down a short definition for it.

1. igneous
2. sedimentary
3. metamorphic
4. mineral
5. crystal
6. lava
7. magma
8. anthracite
9. bituminous
10. coal

Answers will vary.

32

Section 2

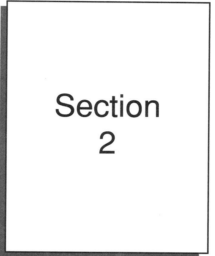

Page 37

Write the rest of the number families. The first one is done for you.

6 x 9 = 54	2. 8 x 7 = 56	6 x 7 = 42
9 x 6 = 54	7 x 8 = 56	7 x 6 = 42
54 ÷ 6 = 9	56 ÷ 8 = 7	42 ÷ 6 = 7
54 ÷ 9 = 6	56 ÷ 7 = 8	42 ÷ 7 = 6
4. 48 ÷ 6 = 8	72 ÷ 8 = 9	6. 6 x 9 = 54	32 ÷ 8 = 4
48 ÷ 8 = 6	72 ÷ 9 = 8	9 x 6 = 54	32 ÷ 4 = 8
6 x 8 = 48	9 x 8 = 72	4 x 8 = 32	
8 x 6 = 48	8 x 9 = 72	54 ÷ 6 = 9	8 x 4 = 32
36 ÷ 4 = 9	9. 9 x 7 = 63	5 x 9 = 45	11. 90 ÷ 9 = 10
36 ÷ 9 = 4	7 x 9 = 63	9 x 5 = 45	90 ÷ 10 = 9
9 x 4 = 36	63 ÷ 9 = 7	45 ÷ 9 = 5	
4 x 9 = 36	63 ÷ 7 = 9	45 ÷ 5 = 9	10 x 9 = 90

Prefixes and Suffixes. Remember: Prefixes are added to the beginning of a base word. Suffixes are added to the end of a base word. Add a prefix to these words. Use mis-, un-, and re-. Write the whole word.

1. happy — **unhappy**
2. spell — **misspell**
3. build — **rebuild**
4. judge — **misjudge**
5. fill — **refill**
6. able — **unable**

Add a suffix to these words. Use -er, -less, -ful, and -ed. Write the whole word.

7. use — **useful, useless**
8. care — **careful, careless**
9. sing — **singer**
10. spell — **spelled, speller**
11. hope — **hopeless, hopeful, hoped**
12. teach — **teacher**
13. paint — **painter, painted**
14. report — **reporter, reported**

Now write two sentences using words of your choice from each of the two word lists above.

1.
2.
Sentences will vary.

37

Page 38

Opinions. Everyone has an opinion on things that happen around them. People will listen to your opinion more often if you state clearly and plainly why you feel as you do.

Write your opinion on one of the following topics or choose one of your own to write about.

1. People should always wear seatbelts.
2. Children should be able to eat anything they want.
3. Schoolchildren should never have homework to do.
4. We should always help other people, whether they are in our country or not.

Answers will vary.

I think kids should be able to choose their own bedtimes!

38

Page 39

Find the product by multiplying.

EXAMPLE:
1. 12 x 4 = 48
2. 22 x 6 = 132
3. 18 x 2 = 36
1 12 x 6 = 72 ... 161
4. 23 x 7 = 161
5. 34 x 6 = 204
6. 16 x 5 = 80
7. 78 x 5 = 390
8. 93 x 6 = 558
9. 86 x 7 = 602
10. 69 x 9 = 621
11. 57 x 4 = 228
12. 62 x 6 = 372
13. 97 x 7 = 679
14. 75 x 8 = 600
15. 33 x 3 = 99
16. 21 x 5 = 105
17. 85 x 8 = 680
18. 68 x 9 = 612
19. 45 x 3 = 135
20. 99 x 9 = 891

Think of your five senses to help you describe the words below. Try to come up with a word for each sense.

	taste	touch	smell	sight	sound
EXAMPLE: fire	smoky	hot	smoky	bright	crackle
candy bar	sweet	smooth	chocolate	brown	crunchy

1. a red rose
2. a rainbow
3. a barnyard
4. a snake's skin
5. rollerblades
6. a snowflake

Sentences will vary.

Choose one of the above and write a paragraph about it. Be very descriptive and put in a lot of details.

Paragraph will vary.

39

Page 40

Prefixes and suffixes can be added to word parts as well as base or root words. Add a prefix or suffix to these word parts, then find and fill in the word shapes below.

1. du plex
2. a d mit
3. don or
4. sel dom
5. pott ery
6. pro gress
7. d i s tant
8. syll able
9. p a n dora
10. gran i te
11. d u plicate
12. a b sent
13. al most
14. fur ious
15. sta t i on

Word shapes:
#7 distant
#1 pandora
#12 absent
#15 progress
#14 admit
#16 undo
#9 furious
#4 duplicate
#8 station
#6 pandora
#13 seldom
#5 granite
#3 syllable
#2 almost
#11 pottery
#10 donor

Mystery Word. Read the following clues to discover the mystery word.

1. The top layer of the earth's surface.
2. It's composed of mineral particles mixed with animal and plant matter.
3. A well-organized, complicated layer of debris covering most of the earth's land surface.
4. It is shallow in some places and deep in other places.
5. It can be very red or very black, as well as other shades and colors.
6. It is one of the most important natural resources of any country.
7. It is so important that we need to make great efforts to conserve it.
8. It takes a long time for it to form.
9. There are different kinds or types.
10. A geologist thinks of it as material that covers the solid rock below the earth's surface.
11. The engineer thinks of it as material on which to build buildings, roads, earth dams, and landing strips.
12. To the farmer and most other people, it is a thin layer of the earth's surface that supports the growth of all kinds of plants.

The Mystery Word is: **soil**

40

117

© Summer Bridge Activities™ 4–5

Page 41

Complete the tables. **Day 3**

1. There are 5 pennies in a nickel.

pennies	5	10	15	20	25	30
nickels	1	2	3	4	5	6

2. There are 10 dimes in a dollar.

dimes	10	20	30	40	50	60
dollars	1	2	3	4	5	6

3. There are 6 cans of pop in each carton.

cans	6	12	18	24	30	36
cartons	1	2	3	4	5	6

4. You can get 6 swimming lessons for $20.

lessons	6	12	18	24	30	36
money	$20	$40	$60	$80	$100	$120

When you write something, your reader should be able to understand clearly what you are trying to say. Read the sentences below and change the underlined word to a more descriptive or exact word.

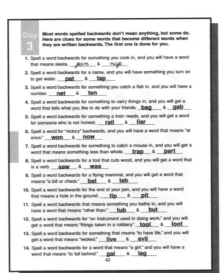

EXAMPLE: This is a good book.
This is an awesome book.

Answers will vary.

1. My teacher is nice. **happy, friendly, pleasant**
2. Your things will be safe here. **bag & coat, books**
3. That is a big building. **huge, enormous, vast**
4. A car went by our house. **zoomed, whizzed, raced**
5. Our pictures of the trip turned out bad. **dark, fuzzy, awful**
6. This is a good sandwich. **delicious, wonderful, awesome**
7. The little boy saw a pretty butterfly. **red & yellow, beautiful**
8. Goliath was a big man. **tall, giant, huge**
9. We had a bad winter. **horrible, awful, depressing**
10. These grapes are awful. **sour, tasteless, rotten**

41

Page 42

Day 3 **Most words spelled backwards don't mean anything, but some do. Here are clues for some words that become different words when they are written backwards. The first one is done for you.**

1. Spell a word backwards for something you cook in, and you will have a word that means siesta. *pan* & *nap*
2. Spell a word backwards for a name, and you will have something you turn on to get water. **pat** & **tap**
3. Spell a word backwards for something you catch a fish in, and you will have a number. **net** & **ten**
4. Spell a word backwards for something to carry things in, and you will get a word that tells what you like to do with your friends. **bag** & **gab**
5. Spell a word backwards for something a train needs, and you will get a word for someone who is not honest. **rail** & **liar**
6. Spell a word for "victory" backwards, and you will have a word that means "at once." **won** & **now**
7. Spell a word backwards for something to catch a mouse in, and you will get a word that means something less than whole. **trap** & **part**
8. Spell a word backwards for a tool that cuts wood, and you will get a word that is a verb. **saw** & **was**
9. Spell a word backwards for a flying mammal, and you will get a word that means "a bill or check." **bat** & **tab**
10. Spell a word backwards for the end of your pen, and you will have a word that means a hole in the ground. **tip** & **pit**
11. Spell a word backwards that means something you bathe in, and you will have a word that means "other than." **tub** & **but**
12. Spell a word backwards for "an instrument used in doing work," and you will get a word that means "things taken in a robbery." **tool** & **loot**
13. Spell a word backwards for something that means "to have life," and you will get a word that means "wicked." **live** & **evil**
14. Spell a word backwards for a word that means "a girl," and you will have a word that means "to fall behind." **gal** & **lag**

42

Page 43

Measuring in Centimeters. Your little finger is about 1 centimeter wide. If you don't have a centimeter tape, use a string and this centimeter ruler to measure for the following activities. **Day 4**

0 1 2 3 4 5 6 7 8 9 10 11 12 13 14 15 16

1. The length of your shoes ________
2. The length and width of this book ________, ________
3. Your neck measurement ________
4. Your waist measurement ________
5. Your kitchen table length and width ________, ________
6. The width of a chair in your home ________
7. Your height in centimeters ________
8. The length of the pencil or pen that you use ________

Answers will vary.

How many other things can you measure? Try estimating, then check to see how close you come to the exact measurement.

Answers will vary.

Underline the pronouns in the following sentences. Remember: A pronoun takes the place of a noun.

1. Will you go with us?
2. He did a good job.
3. She went with me.
4. We ate all of them.
5. It is time for her to go.
6. They will help us today.
7. I thanked him for it.
8. You and I need to hurry.
9. Tomorrow we will go to church.
10. This book came for him.
11. A package came for us.
12. You are a good sport.
13. He and I ate the apples.
14. Animals like them also.
15. It was very good.
16. How did she do?

43

Page 44

Day 4 **The Fourth of July is our nation's birthday. Another name for it is spelled out in the boxes of the puzzle. Finish the puzzle by writing the appropriate words from the firecrackers. You will not use all of the words.**

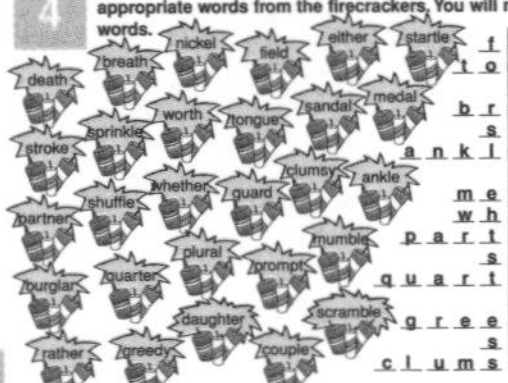

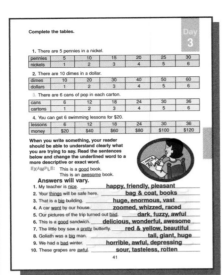

f **I** e l d
t o **N** g u e
D e a t h
b r **E** a t h
s **P** r i n k l e
a n k l **E**
N i c k e l
m e **D** a l
w h **E** t h e r
p a r t **N** e r
s **C** r a m b l e
q u a r t **E** r
g r e e **D** y
s **A** n d a l
c l u m s **Y**

Bugs, Bugs, and More Bugs. The world has so many different kinds of bugs, but there's always room for one more. Create a brand new type of bug. Describe it. Where does it live? What does it do? What does it eat? How does it survive? Who are its friends or enemies?

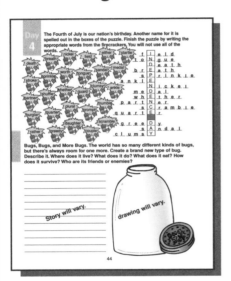

Story will vary.

44

Page 45

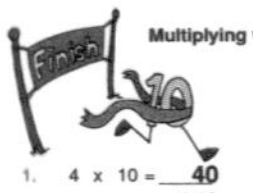

Multiplying with tens and hundreds is fast and fun. **Day 5**

1. 4 x 10 = **40**
2. 600 x 6 = **3600**
3. 7 x 800 = **5,600**
4. 30 x 8 = **240**
5. 5 x 20 = **100**
6. 800 x 5 = **4,000**
7. 8 x 90 = **720**
8. 50 x 6 = **300**
9. 600 x 5 = **3,000**
10. 4 x 100 = **400**
11. 7 x 80 = **560**
12. 7 x 500 = **3,500**
13. 900 x 7 = **6,300**
14. 600 x 4 = **2,400**
15. 900 x 4 = **3,600**
16. 8 x 900 = **7,200**
17. 800 x 2 = **1,600**
18. 7 x 900 = **6,300**
19. 3 x 10 = **30**
20. 700 x 6 = **4,200**
21. 3 x 800 = **2,400**
22. 7 x 40 = **280**
23. 9 x 10 = **90**
24. 10 x 100 = **1,000**
25. 4 x 60 = **240**
26. 80 x 2 = **160**
27. 500 x 4 = **2,000**
28. 7 x 700 = **4900**
29. 30 x 8 = **240**
30. 800 x 6 = **4,800**
31. 9 x 500 = **4500**
30. 9 x 300 = **2700**
33. 300 x 5 = **1,500**

Pronouns such as I, you, he, she, it, we, and they can be the subject of a sentence. Read these sentences. The subject is underlined. Rewrite the sentences and use a subject pronoun in place of the underlined subject. Write in cursive.

1. Jim and I went fishing with our dad.
We went fishing with our dad.
2. The weather was sunny and warm.
It was sunny and warm.
3. Ann and Sue can help us with the bait.
They can help us with the bait.
4. Mr. Jack broke his leg.
He broke his leg.
5. Kathy is going to New York on a vacation.
She is going to New York on a vacation.
6. Ryan will paint the scenery.
He will paint the scenery.

45

Page 46

Day 5 **Categorize these words under one of the headings. Hint: There can be eight words under each heading. Remember: Categorizing words means to put them in groups that have something in common. One row of examples is given.**

interstate	add	region	colony	oxygen	solid
bacteria	city	hemisphere	stop	column	inch
debate	larva	yield	basin	hexagon	canal
environment	speed	equal	fossil	candidate	intersection
measure	insect	bay	caution	map	estimate
numerator	freedom	society	elevation	freeway	railroad
patriot	habitat	civilization	mineral	detour	quotient

Math Words	Geography Words	Transportation Words	Science Words	Social Studies Words
add	*region*	*interstate*	*bacteria*	*colony*
hexagon	**hemisphere**	**caution**	**larva**	**debate**
measure	**bay**	**detour**	**insect**	**freedom**
inch	**map**	**intersection**	**solid**	**candidate**
equal	**basin**	**stop**	**oxygen**	**patriot**
numerator	**canal**	**speed**	**habitat**	**city**
column	**environment**	**yield**	**fossil**	**society**
estimate	**elevation**	**freeway**	**mineral**	**civilization**

What about These Animals in Our Country? Buffalo, condors, and grizzly bears have all but disappeared from our country. The symbol of our country, the bald eagle, is very rare in most states. Bald eagles and bears live in mountainous regions. Prairie dogs and antelope live on the plains. Alligators live in marshy areas. Rattlesnakes live in the desert. Wild turkeys can be found in wilderness areas. These are all animals found in our country. There are also many others. Choose one of the following to do on a separate piece of paper.

1. Choose and draw a picture of an animal from our country. Place it in the correct habitat. Color it accurately. What other interesting animals do you think might belong in this area? Draw them. What other important information does your picture show?
2. If you choose not to draw a picture about an animal, write a paragraph about one. Use the same type of information that the picture would portray.

What animal(s) did you choose?
Answers will vary.

46

Page 47

Addition and multiplication are related. Answer the addition problems and then write the related multiplication problem. **Day 6**

EXAMPLE: 10 + 10 + 10 + 10 + 10 = 50 or 5 x 10 = 50

1. 20 + 20 + 20 = **60** — **3** x **20** = **60**
2. 9 + 9 + 9 + 9 + 9 + 9 = **54** — **6** x **9** = **54**
3. 100 + 100 + 100 + 100 = **400** — **4** x **100** = **400**
4. 8 + 8 + 8 + 8 + 8 + 8 + 8 + 8 = **64** — **8** x **8** = **64**
5. 12 + 12 + 12 + 12 = **48** — **4** x **12** = **48**
6. 75 + 75 + 75 = **225** — **3** x **75** = **225**
7. 35 + 35 + 35 + 35 + 35 + 35 = **210** — **6** x **35** = **210**
8. 51 + 51 + 51 + 51 + 51 = **255** — **5** x **51** = **255**

Use the pronouns me, her, him, it, us, you, and them after action verbs. Use I and me after the other nouns or pronouns. Circle the correct pronoun in each sentence.

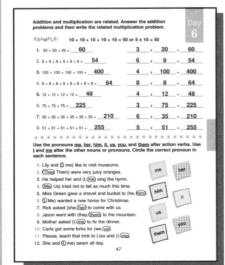

1. Lily and (**I**, me) like to visit museums.
2. (**They**, Them) were very juicy oranges.
3. He helped her and (I, **me**) sing the hymn.
4. (**We**, Us) tried not to fall as much this time.
5. Miss Green gave a shovel and bucket to (he, **him**).
6. (**I**, Me) wanted a new horse for Christmas.
7. Rick asked (she, **her**) to come with us.
8. Jason went with (they, **them**) to the mountain.
9. Mother asked (I, **me**) to fix the dinner.
10. Carla got some forks for (we, **us**).
11. Please, teach that trick to Lisa and (I, **me**).
12. She and (**I**, me) swam all day.

47

Page 48

Day 6 **Study this table about trees, and use it to answer the questions below. Can you identify the trees around you?**

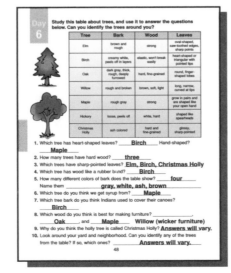

Tree	Bark	Wood	Leaves
Elm	brown and rough	strong	oval-shaped, saw-toothed edges, sharp points
Birch	creamy white, peels off in layers	elastic, won't break easily	heart-shaped or triangular with pointed tips
Oak	dark gray, thick, rough, deeply furrowed	hard, fine-grained	round, finger-shaped lobes
Willow	rough and broken	brown, soft, light	long, narrow, curved at tips
Maple	rough gray	strong	grow in pairs and are shaped like your open hand
Hickory	loose, peels off	white, hard	shaped like spearheads
Christmas Holly	ash colored	hard and fine-grained	glossy, sharp-pointed

1. Which tree has heart-shaped leaves? **Birch** Hand-shaped? **Maple**
2. How many trees have hard wood? **three**
3. Which trees have sharp-pointed leaves? **Elm, Birch, Christmas Holly**
4. Which tree has wood like a rubber band? **Birch**
5. How many different colors of bark does the table show? **four**
Name them **gray, white, ash, brown**
6. Which tree do you think we get syrup from? **Maple**
7. Which tree bark do you think Indians used to cover their canoes? **Birch**
8. Which wood do you think is best for making furniture? ________, **Oak**, and **Maple** **Willow (wicker furniture)**
9. Why do you think the holly tree is called Christmas Holly? **Answers will vary.**
10. Look around your yard and neighborhood. Can you identify any of the trees from the table? If so, which ones? **Answers will vary.**

48

Page 49

Complete this multiplication table. **Day 7**

x	10	20	30	40	50	60	70	80	90
1	10	20	**30**	**40**	**50**	**60**	70	**80**	**90**
2	**20**	**40**	**60**	**80**	**100**	120	**140**	**160**	**180**
3	**30**	60	**90**	**120**	**150**	**180**	**210**	**240**	270
4	**40**	**80**	**120**	160	**200**	**240**	**280**	**320**	**360**
5	**50**	**100**	**150**	**200**	**250**	**300**	350	**400**	**450**
6	**60**	**120**	**180**	**240**	**300**	**360**	**420**	**480**	**540**
7	**70**	**140**	210	**280**	**350**	**420**	**490**	**560**	**630**
8	**80**	**160**	**240**	**320**	**400**	480	**560**	**640**	**720**
9	**90**	**180**	**270**	360	**450**	**540**	**630**	**720**	**810**

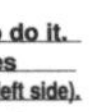

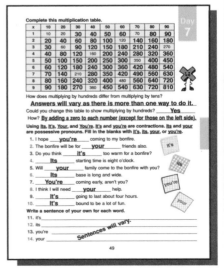

How does multiplying by hundreds differ from multiplying by tens?
Answers will vary as there is more than one way to do it.
Could you change this table to show multiplying by hundreds? **Yes**
How? **By adding a zero to each number (except for those on the left side).**

Using Its, It's, Your, and You're. It's and you're are contractions. Its and your are possessive pronouns. Fill in the blanks with it's, its, your, or you're.

1. I hope **you're** coming to my bonfire.
2. The bonfire will be for **your** friends also.
3. Do you think **it's** too warm for a bonfire?
4. **Its** starting time is eight o'clock.
5. Will **your** family come to the bonfire with you?
6. **Its** base is long and wide.
7. **You're** coming early, aren't you?
8. I think I will need **your** help.
9. **It's** going to last about four hours.
10. **It's** bound to be a lot of fun.

Write a sentence of your own for each word.

11. it's
12. its
13. you're
14. your

Sentences will vary.

49

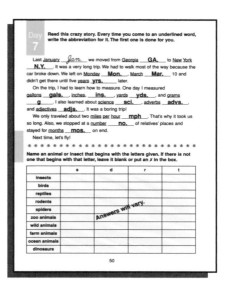

Page 50

Day 7

Read this crazy story. Every time you come to an underlined word, write the abbreviation for it. The first one is done for you.

Last January **Jan.** we moved from Georgia **GA.** to New York **N.Y.** It was a very long trip. We had to walk part of the way because the car broke down. We left on Monday **Mon.**, March **Mar.** 10 and didn't get there until five years **yrs.** later.

On the trip, I had to learn how to measure. One day I measured gallons **gals.**, inches **ins.**, yards **yds.**, and grams **g.** I also learned about science **sci.**, adverbs **advs.**, and adjectives **adjs.** It was a boring trip!

We only traveled about two miles per hour **mph.** That's why it took us so long. Also, we stopped at a number **no.** of relatives' places and stayed for months **mos.** on end.

Next time, let's fly!

Name an animal or insect that begins with the letters given. If there is not one that begins with that letter, leave it blank or put an ✗ in the box.

	s	d	r	t
insects				
birds				
reptiles				
rodents				
spiders				
zoo animals				
wild animals				
farm animals				
ocean animals				
dinosaurs				

Answers will vary.

50

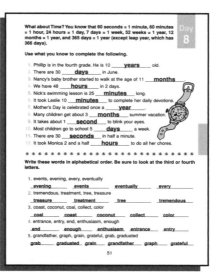

Page 51

Day 8

What about Time? You know that 60 seconds = 1 minute, 60 minutes = 1 hour, 24 hours = 1 day, 7 days = 1 week, 52 weeks = 1 year, 12 months = 1 year, and 365 days = 1 year (except leap year, which has 366 days).

Use what you know to complete the following.

1. Phillip is in the fourth grade. He is 10 **years** old.
2. There are 30 **days** in June.
3. Nancy's baby brother started to walk at the age of 11 **months**.
4. We have 48 **hours** in 2 days.
5. Nick's swimming lesson is 25 **minutes** long.
6. It took Leslie 10 **minutes** to complete her daily devotions.
7. Mother's Day is celebrated once a **year**.
8. Many children get about 3 **months** summer vacation.
9. It takes about 1 **second** to blink your eyes.
10. Most children go to school 5 **days** a week.
11. There are 30 **seconds** in half a minute.
12. It took Monica 2 and a half **hours** to do all her chores.

Write these words in alphabetical order. Be sure to look at the third or fourth letters.

1. events, evening, every, eventually
   evening **events** **eventually** **every**
2. tremendous, treatment, tree, treasure
   treasure **treatment** **tree** **tremendous**
3. coast, coconut, coal, collect, color
   coal **coast** **coconut** **collect** **color**
4. entrance, entry, end, enthusiasm, enough
   end **enough** **enthusiasm** **entrance** **entry**
5. grandfather, graph, grain, grateful, grab, graduated
   grab **graduated** **grain** **grandfather** **graph** **grateful**

51

Page 52

Day 8

What Does It Really Mean? Write what you think these idiomatic expressions mean.

1. She was really pulling my leg. **not telling the truth**
2. Do you think we'll be in hot water? **in trouble**
3. If you don't button your lip, I'll scream! **be quiet**
4. Sonny, please get off my back! **leave me alone**
5. When you are having fun, time flies. **goes fast**
6. You've hit it on the head, Andrew. **got it right**
7. Ryan will lend a hand tomorrow. **help**
8. In the winter, my bedroom is like an icebox. **very cold**
9. Mrs. Tune always has beautiful flowers; she must have a green thumb. **takes good care of plants**
10. My brother's stomach is a bottomless pit. **eats a lot**

A Litter Graph. Go on a "litter" walk. In a plastic bag, gather up litter as you go. Only pick up safe litter. Do not pick up anything marked hazardous waste, needles, or litter you are unsure of. When you are finished, bring it home. Categorize what you have found and display it in a bar graph.

Type of Litter	1	2	3	4	5	6	7	8	9	10	more than 10

Answers will vary.

52

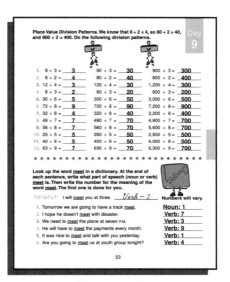

Page 53

Day 9

Place Value Division Patterns. We know that 8 ÷ 2 = 4, so 80 ÷ 2 = 40, and 800 ÷ 2 = 400. Do the following division patterns.

1. 9 ÷ 3 = **3**   90 ÷ 3 = **30**   900 ÷ 3 = **300**
2. 8 ÷ 2 = **4**   80 ÷ 2 = **40**   800 ÷ 2 = **400**
3. 12 ÷ 4 = **3**   120 ÷ 4 = **30**   1,200 ÷ 4 = **300**
4. 6 ÷ 3 = **2**   60 ÷ 3 = **20**   600 ÷ 3 = **200**
5. 30 ÷ 6 = **5**   300 ÷ 6 = **50**   3,000 ÷ 6 = **500**
6. 72 ÷ 8 = **9**   720 ÷ 8 = **90**   7,200 ÷ 8 = **900**
7. 32 ÷ 8 = **4**   320 ÷ 8 = **40**   3,200 ÷ 8 = **400**
8. 49 ÷ 7 = **7**   490 ÷ 7 = **70**   4,900 ÷ 7 = **700**
9. 56 ÷ 8 = **7**   560 ÷ 8 = **70**   5,600 ÷ 8 = **700**
10. 25 ÷ 5 = **5**   250 ÷ 5 = **50**   2,500 ÷ 5 = **500**
11. 40 ÷ 8 = **5**   400 ÷ 8 = **50**   4,000 ÷ 8 = **500**
12. 63 ÷ 9 = **7**   630 ÷ 9 = **70**   6,300 ÷ 9 = **700**

Look up the word meet in a dictionary. At the end of each sentence, write what part of speech (noun or verb) meet is. Then write the number for the meaning of the word meet. The first one is done for you.

EXAMPLE: I will meet you at three. *Verb-7*

Numbers will vary.

1. Tomorrow we are going to have a track meet. **Noun: 1**
2. I hope he doesn't meet with disaster. **Verb: 7**
3. We need to meet the plane at seven P.M. **Verb: 3**
4. He will have to meet the payments every month. **Verb: 9**
5. It was nice to meet and talk with you yesterday. **Verb: 1**
6. Are you going to meet us at youth group tonight? **Verb: 4**

53

Page 54

Day 9

Someone with Strength. What is strength? Choose someone from the Bible known for having amazing strength. Write about this person. How did the person get strength? How did the person use strength? Could the person lose it?

Answers will vary.

54

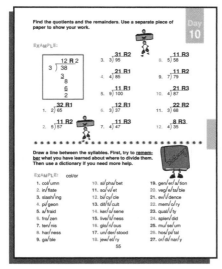

Page 55

Day 10

Find the quotients and the remainders. Use a separate piece of paper to show your work.

EXAMPLE:
```
   12 R 2
 3)38
   3
   8
   6
   2
```

1. 2)65 → **32 R1**
2. 5)57 → **11 R2**
3. 3)95 → **31 R2**
4. 4)85 → **21 R1**
5. 4)100 → **11 R1**
6. 3)37 → **12 R1**
7. 4)47 → **11 R3**
8. 5)58 → **11 R3**
9. 7)79 → **11 R2**
10. 4)87 → **21 R3**
11. 3)68 → **22 R2**
12. 4)35 → **8 R3**

Draw a line between the syllables. First, try to remember what you have learned about where to divide them. Then use a dictionary if you need more help.

EXAMPLE: col/or

1. col/umn
2. in/flate
3. slash/ing
4. pi/geon
5. a/fraid
6. fro/zen
7. ten/nis
8. har/ness
9. ga/ble
10. ai/pha/bet
11. so/vv/et
12. bi/cy/cle
13. dif/fi/cult
14. ker/o/sene
15. live/li/ness
16. glo/ri/ous
17. un/der/stood
18. jew/el/ry
19. gen/er/a/tion
20. veg/e/ta/ble
21. ev/i/dence
22. mem/o/ry
23. quai/i/ty
24. spien/did
25. mu/se/um
26. hos/pi/tal
27. or/di/nar/y

55

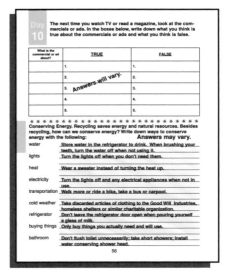

Page 56

Day 10

The next time you watch TV or read a magazine, look at the commercials or ads. In the boxes below, write down what you think is true about the commercials or ads and what you think is false.

What is the commercial or ad about?	TRUE	FALSE
1.	1.	1.
2.	2.	2.
3.	3.	3.
4.	4.	4.
5.	5.	5.

Answers will vary.

Conserving Energy. Recycling saves energy and natural resources. Besides recycling, how can we conserve energy? Write down ways to conserve energy with the following:

Answers may vary.

water — Store water in the refrigerator to drink. When brushing your teeth, turn the water off when not using it.

lights — Turn the lights off when you don't need them.

heat — Wear a sweater instead of turning the heat up.

electricity — Turn the lights off and any electrical appliances when not in use.

transportation — Walk more or ride a bike, take a bus or carpool.

cold weather — Take discarded articles of clothing to the Good Will Industries, homeless shelters or similar charitable organization.

refrigerator — Don't leave the refrigerator door open when pouring yourself a glass of milk.

buying things — Only buy things you actually need and will use.

bathroom — Don't flush toilet unnecessarily; take short showers; install water conserving shower head.

56

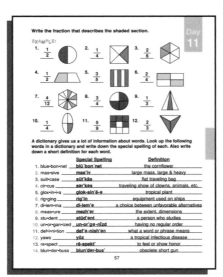

Page 57

Day 11

Write the fraction that describes the shaded section.

EXAMPLE:

1. 1/2
2. 1/4
3. 2/6
4. 1/2
5. 2/3
6. 2/4
7. 4/12
8. 4/8
9. 1/3
10. 1/2
11. 5/6
12. 2/3

A dictionary gives us a lot of information about words. Look up the following words in a dictionary and write down the special spelling of each. Also write down a short definition for each word.

	Special Spelling	Definition
1. blue•bon•net	blü´ bon´net	the cornflower
2. mas•sive	mas´iv	large mass, large & heavy
3. suit•case	süt´kās	flat traveling bag
4. cir•cus	sėr´kәs	traveling show of clowns, animals, etc.
5. glox•in•i•a	glok-sin´ē-ә	tropical plant
6. rig•ging	rig´in	equipment used on ships
7. di•lem•ma	di-lem´ә	a choice between unfavorable alternatives
8. meas•ure	mezh´ėr	the extent, dimensions
9. stu•dent	stüd´ėnt	a person who studies
10. un•or•gan•ized	un-ôr´gә-nīzd	having no regular order
11. def•i•ni•tion	def´ә-nish´әn	what a word or phrase means
12. yaws	yôz	a tropical infectious disease
13. re•spect	rē-spekt´	to feel or show honor
14. blun•der•buss	blun´dėr-bus´	obsolete short gun

57

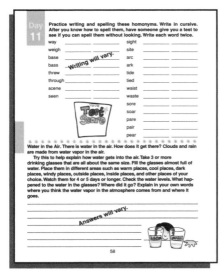

Page 58

Day 11

Practice writing and spelling these homonyms. Write in cursive. After you know how to spell them, have someone give you a test to see if you can spell them without looking. Write each word twice.

way   sight
weigh   site
base   arc
bass   ark
threw   tide
through   tied
scene   waist
seen   waste
             sore
             soar
             pare
             pair
             pear

Writing will vary.

Water in the Air. There is water in the air. How does it get there? Clouds and rain are made from water vapor in the air.

Try this to help explain how water gets into the air. Take 3 or more drinking glasses that are all about the same size. Fill the glasses almost full of water. Place them in different areas such as warm places, cool places, dark places, windy places, outside places, inside places, and other places of your choice. Watch them for 4 or 5 days or longer. Check the water levels. What happened to the water in the glasses? Where did it go? Explain in your own words where you think the water vapor in the atmosphere comes from and where it goes.

Answers will vary.

58

119

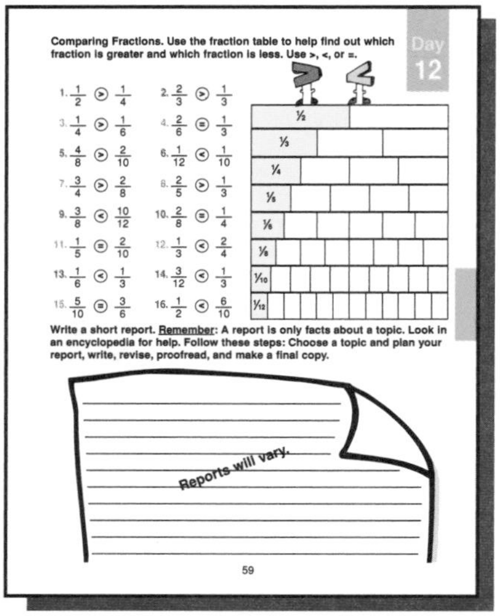
Day 12

Comparing Fractions. Use the fraction table to help find out which fraction is greater and which fraction is less. Use >, <, or =.

1. 1/2 > 1/4   2. 2/3 > 1/3
3. 1/4 > 1/6   4. 2/6 = 1/3
5. 4/8 > 2/10   6. 1/12 < 1/10
7. 3/4 > 2/8   8. 2/5 > 1/3
9. 3/8 < 10/12   10. 2/8 = 1/4
11. 1/5 = 2/10   12. 1/3 < 2/4
13. 1/6 < 1/3   14. 3/12 < 1/3
15. 5/10 = 3/6   16. 1/2 < 6/10

Write a short report. Remember: A report is only facts about a topic. Look in an encyclopedia for help. Follow these steps: Choose a topic and plan your report, write, revise, proofread, and make a final copy.

Reports will vary.

59

Page 59

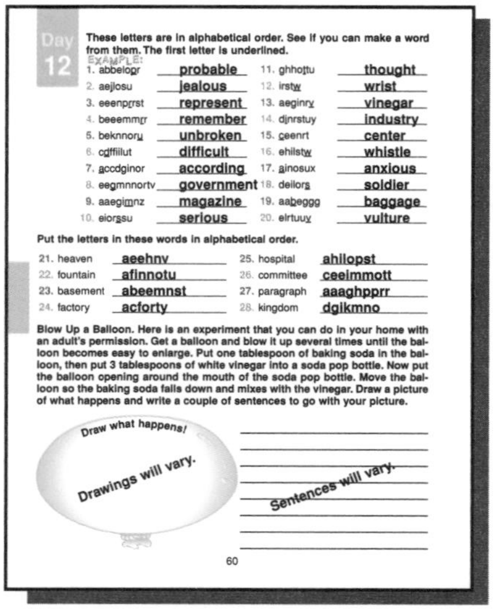
Day 12

These letters are in alphabetical order. See if you can make a word from them. The first letter is underlined.

1. abbelopr	probable	11. ghhottu	thought
2. aejlosu	jealous	12. irstw	wrist
3. eeenprrst	represent	13. aeginrv	vinegar
4. beeemmrr	remember	14. dinrstuy	industry
5. beknnoru	unbroken	15. ceenrt	center
6. cdffiilut	difficult	16. ehilstw	whistle
7. accdginor	according	17. ainosux	anxious
8. eegmnnortv	government	18. deilors	soldier
9. aaegimnz	magazine	19. aabeggg	baggage
10. eiorssu	serious	20. elrtuuv	vulture

Put the letters in these words in alphabetical order.

21. heaven	aeehnv	25. hospital	ahilopst
22. fountain	afinnotu	26. committee	ceeimmott
23. basement	abeemnst	27. paragraph	aaaghpprr
24. factory	acforty	28. kingdom	dgikmno

Blow Up a Balloon. Here is an experiment that you can do in your home with an adult's permission. Get a balloon and blow it up several times until the balloon becomes easy to enlarge. Put one tablespoon of baking soda in the balloon, then put 3 tablespoons of white vinegar into a soda pop bottle. Now put the balloon opening around the mouth of the soda pop bottle. Move the balloon so the baking soda falls down and mixes with the vinegar. Draw a picture of what happens and write a couple of sentences to go with your picture.

Draw what happens!

Drawings will vary.

Sentences will vary.

60

Page 60

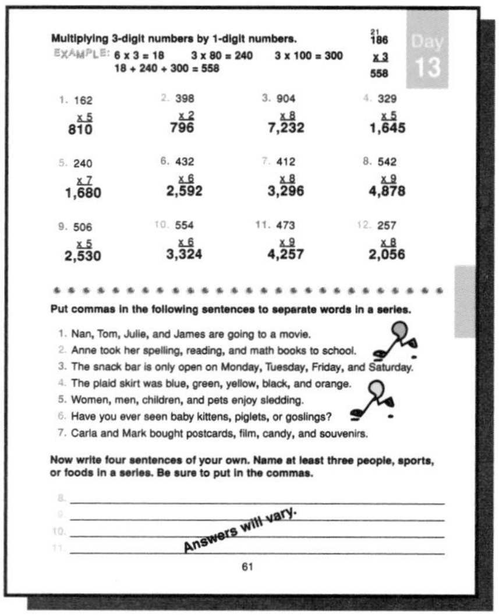
Day 13

Multiplying 3-digit numbers by 1-digit numbers.

EXAMPLE: 6 x 3 = 18   3 x 80 = 240   3 x 100 = 300   186 x 3 = 558
18 + 240 + 300 = 558

1. 162 x 5 = 810	2. 398 x 2 = 796	3. 904 x 8 = 7,232	4. 329 x 5 = 1,645
5. 240 x 7 = 1,680	6. 432 x 6 = 2,592	7. 412 x 8 = 3,296	8. 542 x 9 = 4,878
9. 506 x 5 = 2,530	10. 554 x 6 = 3,324	11. 473 x 9 = 4,257	12. 257 x 8 = 2,056

Put commas in the following sentences to separate words in a series.

1. Nan, Tom, Julie, and James are going to a movie.
2. Anne took her spelling, reading, and math books to school.
3. The snack bar is only open on Monday, Tuesday, Friday, and Saturday.
4. The plaid skirt was blue, green, yellow, black, and orange.
5. Women, men, children, and pets enjoy sledding.
6. Have you ever seen baby kittens, piglets, or goslings?
7. Carla and Mark bought postcards, film, candy, and souvenirs.

Now write four sentences of your own. Name at least three people, sports, or foods in a series. Be sure to put in the commas.

8.
9.
10.
11.

Answers will vary.

61

Page 61

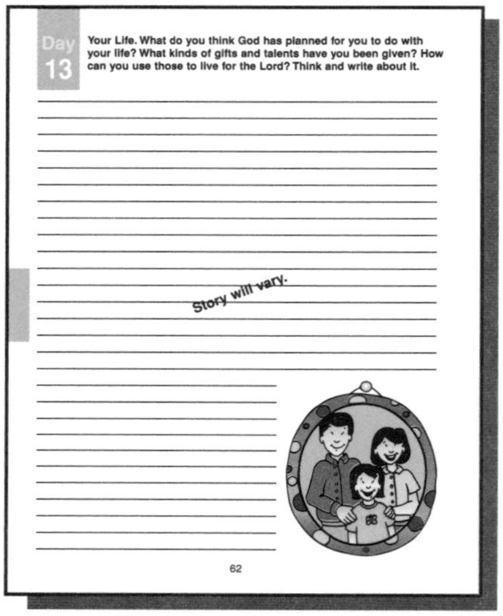
Day 13

Your Life. What do you think God has planned for you to do with your life? What kinds of gifts and talents have you been given? How can you use those to live for the Lord? Think and write about it.

Story will vary.

62

Page 62

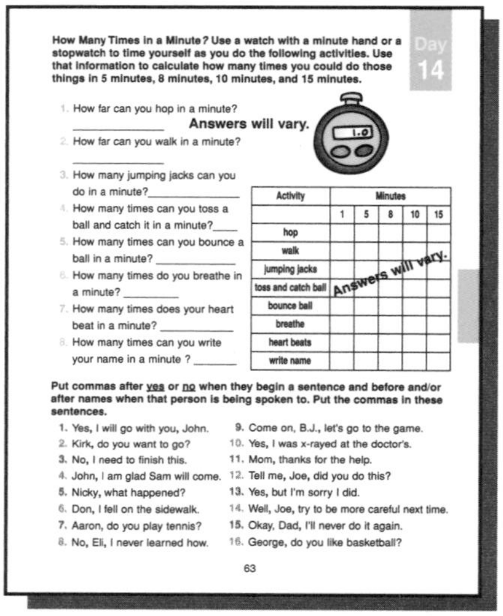
Day 14

How Many Times in a Minute? Use a watch with a minute hand or a stopwatch to time yourself as you do the following activities. Use that information to calculate how many times you could do those things in 5 minutes, 8 minutes, 10 minutes, and 15 minutes.

1. How far can you hop in a minute?
Answers will vary.
2. How far can you walk in a minute?
3. How many jumping jacks can you do in a minute?
4. How many times can you toss a ball and catch it in a minute?
5. How many times can you bounce a ball in a minute?
6. How many times do you breathe in a minute?
7. How many times does your heart beat in a minute?
8. How many times can you write your name in a minute?

Activity	Minutes				
	1	5	8	10	15
hop					
walk					
jumping jacks					
toss and catch ball	Answers will vary.				
bounce ball					
breathe					
heart beats					
write name					

Put commas after yes or no when they begin a sentence and before and/or after names when that person is being spoken to. Put the commas in these sentences.

1. Yes, I will go with you, John.
2. Kirk, do you want to go?
3. No, I need to finish this.
4. John, I am glad Sam will come.
5. Nicky, what happened?
6. Don, I fell on the sidewalk.
7. Aaron, do you play tennis?
8. No, Eli, I never learned how.
9. Come on, B.J., let's go to the game.
10. Yes, I was x-rayed at the doctor's.
11. Mom, thanks for the help.
12. Tell me, Joe, did you do this?
13. Yes, but I'm sorry I did.
14. Well, Joe, try to be more careful next time.
15. Okay, Dad, I'll never do it again.
16. George, do you like basketball?

63

Page 63

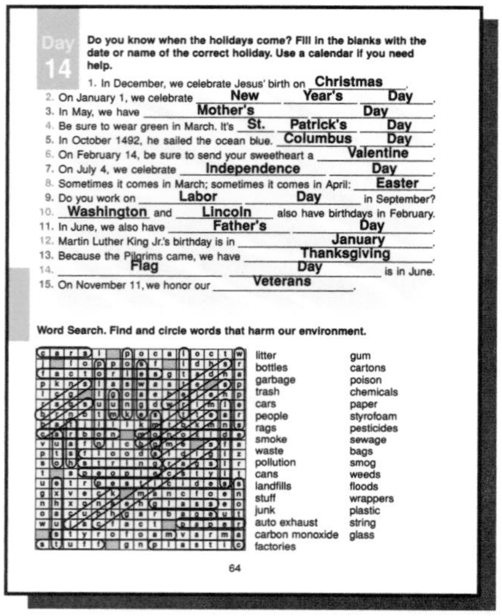
Day 14

Do you know when the holidays come? Fill in the blanks with the date or name of the correct holiday. Use a calendar if you need help.

1. In December, we celebrate Jesus' birth on Christmas.
2. On January 1, we celebrate New Year's Day.
3. In May, we have Mother's Day.
4. Be sure to wear green in March. It's St. Patrick's Day.
5. In October 1492, he sailed the ocean blue. Columbus Day
6. On February 14, be sure to send your sweetheart a Valentine.
7. On July 4, we celebrate Independence Day.
8. Sometimes it comes in March; sometimes it comes in April: Easter.
9. Do you work on Labor Day in September?
10. Washington and Lincoln also have birthdays in February.
11. In June, we also have Father's Day.
12. Martin Luther King Jr.'s birthday is in January.
13. Because the Pilgrims came, we have Thanksgiving Day.
14. Flag Day is in June.
15. On November 11, we honor our Veterans.

Word Search. Find and circle words that harm our environment.

litter, bottles, garbage, trash, cars, people, rags, smoke, waste, pollution, cans, landfills, stuff, junk, auto exhaust, carbon monoxide, factories, gum, cartons, poison, chemicals, paper, styrofoam, pesticides, sewage, bags, smog, weeds, floods, wrappers, plastic, string, glass

64

Page 64

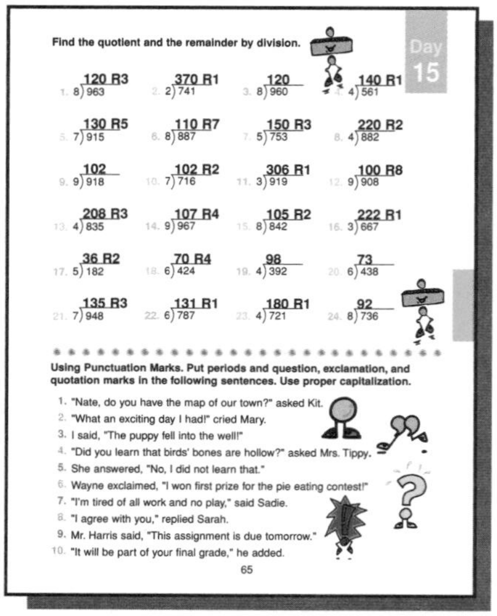
Day 15

Find the quotient and the remainder by division.

1. 963 ÷ 8 = 120 R3	2. 741 ÷ 2 = 370 R1	3. 960 ÷ 8 = 120	4. 561 ÷ 4 = 140 R1
5. 915 ÷ 7 = 130 R5	6. 887 ÷ 8 = 110 R7	7. 753 ÷ 5 = 150 R3	8. 882 ÷ 4 = 220 R2
9. 918 ÷ 9 = 102	10. 716 ÷ 7 = 102 R2	11. 919 ÷ 3 = 306 R1	12. 908 ÷ 9 = 100 R8
13. 835 ÷ 4 = 208 R3	14. 967 ÷ 9 = 107 R4	15. 842 ÷ 8 = 105 R2	16. 667 ÷ 3 = 222 R1
17. 182 ÷ 5 = 36 R2	18. 424 ÷ 6 = 70 R4	19. 392 ÷ 4 = 98	20. 438 ÷ 6 = 73
21. 948 ÷ 7 = 135 R3	22. 787 ÷ 6 = 131 R1	23. 721 ÷ 4 = 180 R1	24. 736 ÷ 8 = 92

Using Punctuation Marks. Put periods and question, exclamation, and quotation marks in the following sentences. Use proper capitalization.

1. "Nate, do you have the map of our town?" asked Kit.
2. "What an exciting day I had!" cried Mary.
3. I said, "The puppy fell into the well!"
4. "Did you learn that birds' bones are hollow?" asked Mrs. Tippy.
5. She answered, "No, I did not learn that."
6. Wayne exclaimed, "I won first prize for the pie eating contest!"
7. "I'm tired of all work and no play," said Sadie.
8. "I agree with you," replied Sarah.
9. Mr. Harris said, "This assignment is due tomorrow."
10. "It will be part of your final grade," he added.

65

Page 65

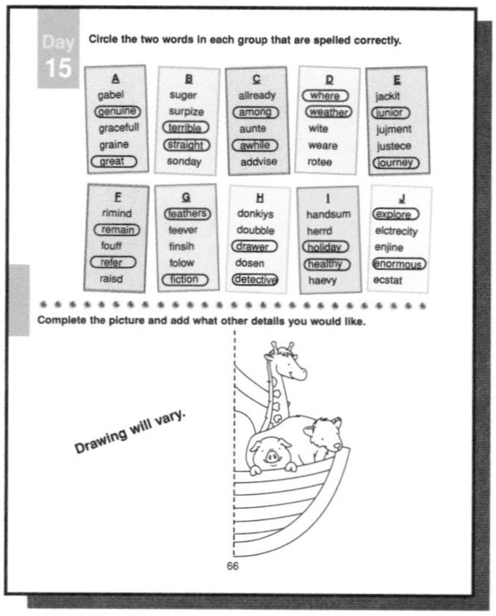
Day 15

Circle the two words in each group that are spelled correctly.

A	B	C	D	E
gabel	suger	allready	(where)	jackit
(genuine)	surpize	(among)	(weather)	(junior)
gracefull	(terrible)	aunte	wite	jujment
graine	(straight)	(awhile)	weare	justece
(great)	sonday	addvise	rotee	(journey)

F	G	H	I	J
rimind	(feathers)	donkiys	handsum	(explore)
(remain)	feever	doubble	herrd	elctrecity
fouff	finsih	(drawer)	(holiday)	enjine
(refer)	folow	dosen	(healthy)	(enormous)
raisd	(fiction)	(detective)	haevy	ecstat

Complete the picture and add what other details you would like.

Drawing will vary.

66

Page 66

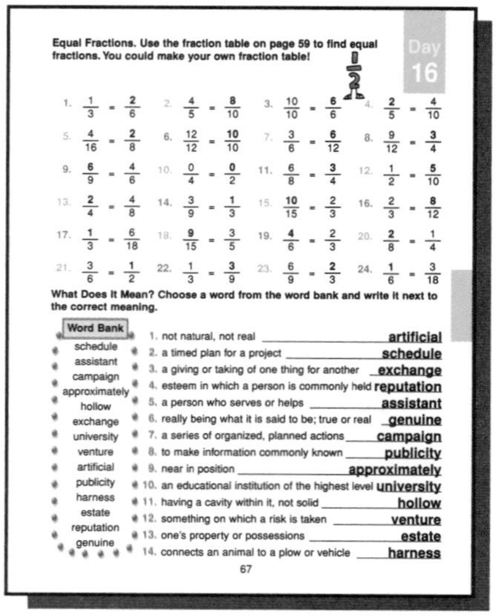
Day 16

Equal Fractions. Use the fraction table on page 59 to find equal fractions. You could make your own fraction table!

1. 1/3 = 2/6	2. 4/5 = 8/10	3. 10/10 = 6/6	4. 2/5 = 4/10
5. 4/16 = 2/8	6. 12/12 = 10/10	7. 3/6 = 6/12	8. 9/12 = 3/4
9. 6/9 = 4/6	10. 0/4 = 0/2	11. 6/8 = 3/4	12. 1/2 = 5/10
13. 2/4 = 4/8	14. 3/9 = 1/3	15. 10/15 = 2/3	16. 2/3 = 8/12
17. 1/3 = 6/18	18. 9/15 = 3/5	19. 4/6 = 2/3	20. 2/8 = 1/4
21. 3/6 = 1/2	22. 1/3 = 3/9	23. 6/9 = 2/3	24. 1/6 = 3/18

What Does It Mean? Choose a word from the word bank and write it next to the correct meaning.

Word Bank: schedule, assistant, campaign, approximately, hollow, exchange, university, venture, artificial, publicity, harness, estate, reputation, genuine

1. not natural, not real artificial
2. a timed plan for a project schedule
3. a giving or taking of one thing for another exchange
4. esteem in which a person is commonly held reputation
5. a person who serves or helps assistant
6. really being what it is said to be; true or real genuine
7. a series of organized, planned actions campaign
8. to make information commonly known publicity
9. near in position approximately
10. an educational institution of the highest level university
11. having a cavity within it, not solid hollow
12. something on which a risk is taken venture
13. one's property or possessions estate
14. connects an animal to a plow or vehicle harness

67

Page 67

Page 68

Look at the homonyms you spelled on page 58. Choose five pairs of these and write a sentence for each one.

EXAMPLE: way/weigh
I could not see him; we were **way** down the road.
How much do you **weigh**?

1. _____
2. _____
3. _____   *Sentences will vary.*
4. _____
5. _____

First-Aid Kit. Every home should have a first-aid kit. This enables the family to have many types of bandages and medicines in one place, should they be needed.

Make a list of things you think should be in a first-aid kit. When you are finished, check with your parents to see if you have all the basic things listed for a first-aid kit. If your family has one, ask your parents to go through it with you.

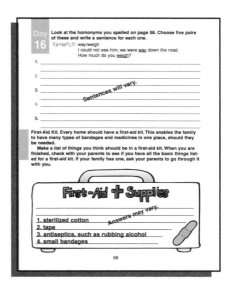

First-Aid + Supplies

1. sterilized cotton   *Answers may vary.*
2. tape
3. antiseptics, such as rubbing alcohol
4. small bandages

68

Page 69

Adding Fractions.

$\frac{2}{3} + \frac{1}{3} = \frac{3}{3}$ ← add the numerator
use the same denominator

1. $\frac{1}{3} + \frac{1}{3} = \frac{2}{3}$ 2. $\frac{1}{2} + \frac{1}{2} = \frac{2}{2}$ 3. $\frac{6}{12} + \frac{5}{12} = \frac{11}{12}$ 4. $\frac{6}{12} + \frac{7}{12} = \frac{13}{12}$

5. $\frac{5}{8} + \frac{2}{8} = \frac{7}{8}$ 6. $\frac{2}{10} + \frac{7}{10} = \frac{9}{10}$ 7. $\frac{6}{12} + \frac{5}{12} = \frac{11}{12}$ 8. $\frac{11}{12} + \frac{11}{12} = \frac{22}{12}$

9. $\frac{7}{10} + \frac{1}{10} = \frac{8}{10}$ 10. $\frac{1}{6} + \frac{5}{6} = \frac{6}{6}$ 11. $\frac{4}{9} + \frac{4}{9} = \frac{8}{9}$ 12. $\frac{6}{10} + \frac{7}{10} = \frac{13}{10}$

13. $\frac{1}{4} + \frac{1}{4} = \frac{2}{4}$ 14. $\frac{4}{10} + \frac{5}{10} = \frac{9}{10}$ 15. $\frac{3}{8} + \frac{5}{8} = \frac{8}{8}$ 16. $\frac{2}{8} + \frac{4}{8} = \frac{6}{8}$

17. $\frac{3}{6} + \frac{1}{6} = \frac{4}{6}$ 18. $\frac{6}{12} + \frac{5}{12} = \frac{11}{12}$ 19. $\frac{2}{8} + \frac{1}{8} = \frac{3}{8}$ 20. $\frac{8}{12} + \frac{5}{12} = \frac{13}{12}$

21. $\frac{3}{12} + \frac{11}{12} = \frac{14}{12}$ 22. $\frac{5}{10} + \frac{5}{10} = \frac{10}{10}$ 23. $\frac{3}{8} + \frac{4}{8} = \frac{7}{8}$

Circle the abbreviations and titles in these sentences. **Remember:** Abbreviations are short forms of words and usually begin with capital letters and end with periods.

1. (Dr.) Cox is my family doctor.
2. Do you live on Rocksberry (Rd.)?
3. My teacher's name is (Ms.) Hansen.
4. On (Mon.) we are taking a trip to Fort Worth, (Tx.)
5. Will (Mr.) Harris teach your Sunday school class?
6. Rick's birthday and mine are both on (Feb.) 16.

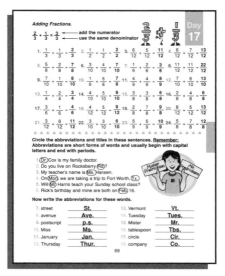

Now write the abbreviations for these words.

7. street	**St.**	13. Vermont	**Vt.**
8. avenue	**Ave.**	14. Tuesday	**Tues.**
9. postscript	**p.s.**	15. Mister	**Mr.**
10. Miss	**Ms.**	16. tablespoon	**Tbs.**
11. January	**Jan.**	17. circle	**Cir.**
12. Thursday	**Thur.**	18. company	**Co.**

69

Page 70

Choose 4 **compound** words and illustrate them.

EXAMPLE: <u>drawbridge</u> is <u>draw</u> and <u>bridge</u>.

Here are some to choose from, or you can choose some of your own: billfold, screwdriver, backyard, butterfly, rainbow, supermarket, postman, undertake, windpipe, starfish, basketball.

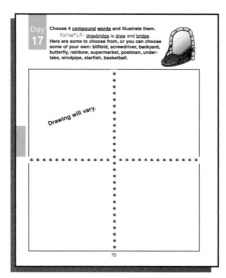

Drawing will vary.

70

Page 71

Understanding Polygons.

Closed figures that have straight lines are *polygons*. Which of these are polygons? **1, 3, 4, 5**

1. [square]   2. [circle]   3. [triangle]   4. [parallelogram]   5. [diamond]

Why? <u>Because they have straight lines and they are closed shapes.</u>

Where each side or point meets is called a *vertex*. Count and write the number of sides and the number of vertices each polygon has.

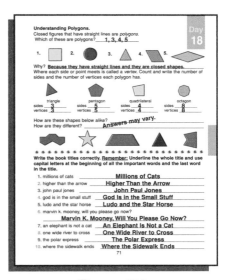

triangle	pentagon	quadrilateral	octagon
sides **3**	sides **5**	sides **4**	sides **8**
vertices **3**	vertices **5**	vertices **4**	vertices **8**

How are these shapes below alike?
How are they different? *Answers may vary.*

Write the book titles correctly. **Remember:** Underline the whole title and use capital letters at the beginning of all the important words and the last word in the title.

1. millions of cats	**Millions of Cats**
2. higher than the arrow	**Higher Than the Arrow**
3. john paul jones	**John Paul Jones**
4. god is in the small stuff	**God Is in the Small Stuff**
5. ludo and the star horse	**Ludo and the Star Horse**
6. marvin k. mooney, will you please go now?	**Marvin K. Mooney, Will You Please Go Now?**
7. an elephant is not a cat	**An Elephant Is Not a Cat**
8. one wide river to cross	**One Wide River to Cross**
9. the polar express	**The Polar Express**
10. where the sidewalk ends	**Where the Sidewalk Ends**

71

Page 72

Neighborhood Survey. Conduct a survey with your neighborhood, friends, or relatives. Find out how many have pets. If possible, observe them with their pets. Do they keep their pets inside or outside? Are the pets left to find their own food, or is their food provided for them? How much space do they have to move around in? In what condition are their pets? Think of other questions you might ask. Record your information in a report, chart, graph, table, or picture.

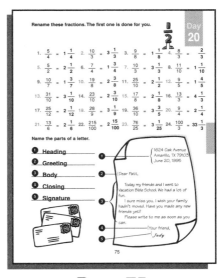

Writing will vary.

72

Page 73

Use what you know about polygons to make a pattern. Start with one polygon and flip, turn, or slide it to make a pattern.

EXAMPLE:

Now try your hand at making some polygon patterns.

Drawing will vary.

Review of Homonyms or Homophones. Write 10 sentences using some of these pairs of homonyms or homophones. Be sure to use both words and underline the homonyms you use.

EXAMPLE: <u>Would</u> you chop some <u>wood</u>?

1. no, know
2. ate, eight
3. see, sea
4. knight, night
5. new, knew
6. four, for
7. sun, son
8. tail, tale
9. sale, sail
10. so, sew
11. way, weigh
12. sent, cent
13. rode, road
14. pair, pear
15. their, there
16. hour, our
17. red, read
18. wear, where

Sentences will vary.

Here are some examples:
1. My sailboat is for <u>sale</u>.
2. I <u>knew</u> I needed to practice the <u>new</u> words.
3. Their house is over <u>there</u>.
4. Where is the shirt I'm going to <u>wear</u>?
5. <u>No</u>, I don't <u>know</u> how to ride a bike!

73

Page 74

Read this paragraph. Put in the punctuation marks that are missing. Don't forget capitals.

Do you ever wonder about the planet Pluto? It takes Pluto 248 Earth years to orbit the sun. Most of the time, Pluto is farther away from the sun than any other planet. But for some time, Pluto had been closer to the sun than Neptune because it was traveling inside Neptune's orbit. It remained in Neptune's orbit until February 9, 1999. Pluto is now traveling out of Neptune's orbit.

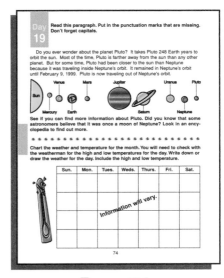

Sun Mercury Venus Earth Mars Jupiter Saturn Uranus Neptune Pluto

See if you can find more information about Pluto. Did you know that some astronomers believe that it was once a moon of Neptune? Look in an encyclopedia to find out more.

Chart the weather and temperature for the month. You will need to check with the weatherman for the high and low temperatures for the day. Write down or draw the weather for the day. Include the high and low temperature.

Sun.	Mon.	Tues.	Weds.	Thurs.	Fri.	Sat.
			Information will vary.			

74

Page 75

Rename these fractions. The first one is done for you.

1. $\frac{5}{4} = 1\frac{1}{4}$ 2. $\frac{10}{3} = 3\frac{1}{3}$ 3. $\frac{9}{8} = 1\frac{1}{8}$ 4. $\frac{5}{3} = 1\frac{2}{3}$

5. $\frac{5}{2} = 2\frac{1}{2}$ 6. $\frac{7}{4} = 1\frac{3}{4}$ 7. $\frac{10}{3} = 3\frac{1}{3}$ 8. $\frac{11}{10} = 1\frac{1}{10}$

9. $\frac{10}{7} = 1\frac{3}{7}$ 10. $\frac{19}{8} = 2\frac{3}{8}$ 11. $\frac{25}{12} = 2\frac{1}{12}$ 12. $\frac{9}{5} = 1\frac{4}{5}$

13. $\frac{31}{10} = 3\frac{1}{10}$ 14. $\frac{23}{10} = 2\frac{3}{10}$ 15. $\frac{17}{8} = 2\frac{1}{8}$ 16. $\frac{13}{4} = 3\frac{1}{4}$

17. $\frac{25}{12} = 2\frac{1}{12}$ 18. $\frac{28}{9} = 3\frac{1}{9}$ 19. $\frac{36}{5} = 7\frac{1}{5}$ 20. $\frac{22}{4} = 5\frac{1}{2}$

21. $\frac{13}{6} = 2\frac{1}{6}$ 22. $\frac{215}{100} = 2\frac{15}{100}$ 23. $\frac{76}{25} = 3\frac{1}{25}$ 24. $\frac{100}{3} = 33\frac{1}{3}$

Name the parts of a letter.

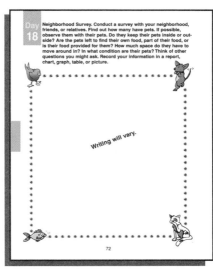

❶ Heading
❷ Greeting
❸ Body
❹ Closing
❺ Signature

1624 Oak Avenue
Amarillo, TX 79102
June 20, 1995

Dear Patti,

Today my friends and I went to Vacation Bible School. We had a lot of fun.

I sure miss you. I wish your family hadn't moved. Have you made any new friends yet?

Please write to me as soon as you can.

Your friend,
Jody

75

Page 76

Complete each sentence by circling the word that is spelled correctly, then write it in the blank space. Use a dictionary if necessary.

1. Shadrach, Meshach, and Abednego were able to **escape** from harm.
   (a.) escape   b. iscape   c. eskape   d. acape   e. iccape
2. Mother paid $100.00 for **groceries**
   a. groseries   b. groceeries   (c.) groceries   d. grceress   e. grooseries
3. Anna is a very **creative** person.
   a. kreative   (b.) creative   c. creeative   d. crative   e. creetive
4. Have you ever seen a more **handsome** man?
   a. handsum   b. hansome   c. handsoome   d. handcome   (e.) handsome
5. We love to **sleigh** ride in the winter.
   (a.) sleigh   b. sleia   c. cleigh   d. slagh   e. sleiegh
6. I found the perfect **material** for my new dress.
   (a.) material   b. materiel   c. materiel   d. materail   e. materiall
7. Scott's son got a **scholarship** to Harvard University.
   a. scholarchip   (b.) scholarship   c. skullarship   d. scholarsip   e. scholarship
8. What would it take to **satisfy** your appetite?
   a. satesfy   b. satisfi   (c.) satisfy   d. satisfy   e. satisfey
9. Richard, turn down the **volume**
   a. volume   b. vollume   (c.) volume   d. volumme   e. volumee
10. That was a **fantastic** report, Army.
    a. fantistic   b. fantastik   c. fantastic   (d.) fantastic   e. fantastic
11. We saw a man fight an **alligator** in the show.
    a. aligator   (b.) alligator   c. allegator   d. alligator   e. aligater
12. Do you understand the **instructions**?
    (a.) instructions   b. instructions   c. instructions   d. instructions   e. instractions

Electricity. Make a list of all the things around you that use electricity.

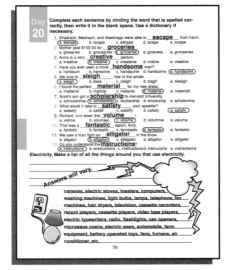

Answers will vary.

cameras, electric stoves, toasters, computers, washing machines, light bulbs, lamps, telephone, fax machines, hair dryers, television, cassette recorders, record players, cassette players, video tape players, electric typewriters, radio, flashlights, can openers, microwave ovens, electric saws, automobile, farm equipment, battery operated toys, fans, furnace, air conditioner, etc.

76

Section 3

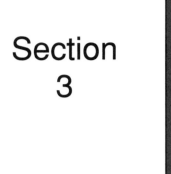

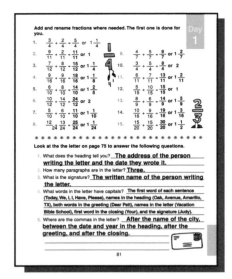

Page 81

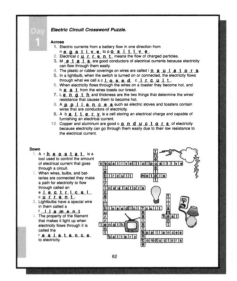

Page 82

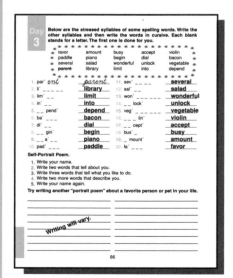

Page 83

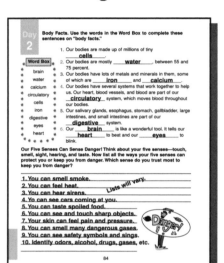

Page 84

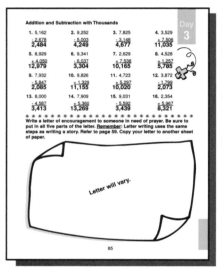

Page 85

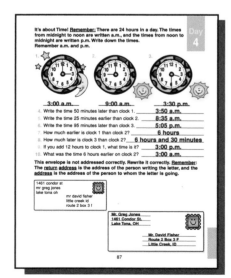

Page 86

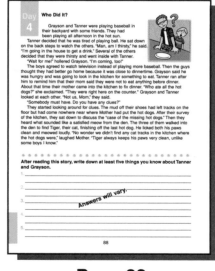

Page 87

Page 88

Page 89

Fractions to Tenths and the Decimal Equivalents for the Fraction.
Remember: When working with fractions that have a denominator of 10, you can write them as fractions in tenths, or you can use the decimal equivalent. Do this activity by writing each both ways.

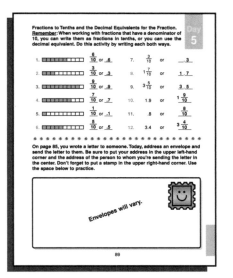

1. ▯▯▯▯▯▯▯ $\frac{6}{10}$ or .6
2. ▯▯▯ $\frac{3}{10}$ or .3
3. ▯▯▯▯▯▯▯▯▯ $\frac{9}{10}$ or .9
4. ▯▯▯▯▯▯▯ $\frac{7}{10}$ or .7
5. ▯ $\frac{1}{10}$ or .1
6. ▯▯▯▯▯ $\frac{5}{10}$ or .5

7. $\frac{3}{10}$ or .3
8. $1\frac{7}{10}$ or 1.7
9. $3\frac{5}{10}$ or 3.5
10. 1.9 or $1\frac{9}{10}$
11. .8 or $\frac{8}{10}$
12. 3.4 or $3\frac{4}{10}$

On page 85, you wrote a letter to someone. Today, address an envelope and send the letter to them. Be sure to put your address in the upper left-hand corner and the address of the person to whom you're sending the letter in the center. Don't forget to put a stamp in the upper right-hand corner. Use the space below to practice.

Envelopes will vary.

89

Page 90

Write an analogy to finish these sentences. Remember: An analogy is a comparison between two pairs of words. Try to think of the relationship between the two words given and then think of another word that has the same kind of relationship to the third word.
EXAMPLE: Story is to read as song is to sing.

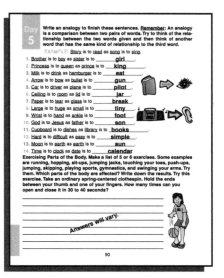

1. Brother is to boy as sister is to **girl**.
2. Princess is to queen as prince is to **king**.
3. Milk is to drink as hamburger is to **eat**.
4. Arrow is to bow as bullet is to **gun**.
5. Car is to driver as plane is to **pilot**.
6. Ceiling is to room as lid is to **jar**.
7. Paper is to tear as glass is to **break**.
8. Large is to huge as small is to **tiny**.
9. Wrist is to hand as ankle is to **foot**.
10. God is to Jesus as father is to **son**.
11. Cupboard is to dishes as library is to **books**.
12. Hard is to difficult as easy is to **simple**.
13. Moon is to earth as earth is to **sun**.
14. Time is to clock as date is to **calendar**.

Exercising Parts of the Body. Make a list of 5 or 6 exercises. Some examples are running, hopping, sit-ups, jumping jacks, touching your toes, push-ups, jumping, skipping, playing sports, gymnastics, and swinging your arms. Try them. Which parts of the body are affected? Write down the results. Try this exercise. Take an ordinary spring-centered clothespin. Hold the ends between your thumb and one of your fingers. How many times can you open and close it in 30 to 40 seconds?

Answers will vary.

90

Page 91

Use what you know about fractions to tenths and their decimal equivalents to work with hundreds. Remember: When a whole object is divided into 100 equal parts, each part is one hundredth (1/100 or .01). Write the fraction as a decimal. The first one is done for you.

1. $\frac{49}{100}$ .49
2. $\frac{25}{100}$ .25
3. $\frac{20}{100}$ .20
4. $\frac{52}{100}$ .52
5. $\frac{86}{100}$ .86
6. $\frac{37}{100}$ .37
7. $\frac{4}{100}$ .04
8. $\frac{9}{100}$ .09

Now write the mixed number as a decimal.

9. $1\frac{93}{100}$ 1.93
10. $7\frac{15}{100}$ 7.15
11. $9\frac{13}{100}$ 9.13
12. $15\frac{47}{100}$ 15.47
13. $46\frac{89}{100}$ 46.89
14. $35\frac{6}{100}$ 35.06
15. $94\frac{7}{100}$ 94.07
16. $625\frac{12}{100}$ 625.12
17. $12\frac{5}{100}$ 12.05
18. $81\frac{1}{100}$ 81.01
19. $37\frac{87}{100}$ 37.87
20. $10\frac{11}{100}$ 10.11

Adjectives are words that tell about or describe nouns and pronouns. Circle the adjective(s) in these sentences. Write the noun(s) or pronoun(s) described at the end of the sentence. The first one is done for you.

1. A (beautiful) light flashed across the (cloudy) sky. *light   sky*
2. Her (golden) hair was very (long). **hair**
3. On the (tall) mountain we found (blue) and (yellow) flowers. **mountain, flowers**
4. Daniel was (brave) while he was in the lions' den. **He**
5. It is (fun) but it is also (dangerous) to skydive. **It, it, skydive**
6. Our (brown) dog had (six) (cute) puppies. **dog, puppies**

Now fill in the blanks with adjectives.

7. My _____ pencil is never in my desk.
8. The _____ students were having a _____ time.
9. Lions are _____ animals that we can see in the zoo.
10. The *Answers will vary.* _____ ride was making me sick.
11. My brother, Jack, sang a _____ song when we were camping.
12. _____, _____ snakes were wiggling around in the box.

91

Page 92

Maintaining Good Health. Fill in the blanks with the following health terms: nutrients, healthy, sleep, exercise, liquids, water, cleanliness, checkups, energy, food groups.

1. **Nutrients** are basic nourishing ingredients in good foods that we eat.
2. **Exercise** helps us to strengthen our muscles. It helps our heart and lungs grow, too.
3. **Checkups** help us prevent tooth decay and maintain good health.
4. Meat, fruits and vegetables, milk, and breads and cereals make up the basic four **food groups** that keep us healthy.
5. Being healthy means feeling good and having the **energy** to work and play.
6. Vitamins and minerals are kinds of **nutrients** that we get from food.
7. Being **healthy** means feeling good and not being sick.
8. Sugar, starch, and fats are **nutrients** that the body uses for fuel to give us **energy**.
9. We need to drink a lot of **liquid** because our body is approximately 55–75% **water**.
10. Plenty of **sleep** helps give our body time to grow and repair itself. Children need 10 to 11 hours of it because they are not finished growing.
11. **Cleanliness** is a way of fighting germs and staying healthy.
12. We need health **checkups** by a doctor or dentist at least once a year.

Are You Confused?

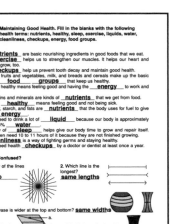

1. Are any of the lines curved? **no**
2. Which line is the longest? **same lengths**
3. Which vase is wider at the top and bottom? **same widths**
4. Which line is longer, a or b? **same length**
5. Is the hat taller than it is wide? **Both same size**

92

Page 93

Decimals and Money. Remember: 100 pennies = 1 dollar. One penny is 1/100 of a dollar, or $.01, so 49 pennies = $.49. We can compute money by adding, subtracting, multiplying, and dividing—just watch the decimals. Look at the signs. Use a separate piece of paper to show your work.

EXAMPLE:
```
 $57.34      $62.89      $12.45       $3.95
+62.89      -34.91      x    3     5 )$19.75
$120.23      $27.98      $37.35
```

1. $409.75 − 249.83 = **$159.92**
2. $14.74 x 3 = **$44.22**
3. $492.00 − 349.50 = **$142.50**
4. 4)$12.92 = **$3.23**
5. $162.49 + 186.32 = **$348.81**
6. 7)$49.77 = **$7.11**
7. $601.89 + 403.23 = **$1,005.12**
8. $9.57 x 6 = **$57.42**
9. $668.45 + 171.63 = **$840.08**
10. $915.04 − 102.56 = **$812.48**
11. $741.13 x 8 = **$5,929.04**
12. 4)$29.48 = **$7.37**

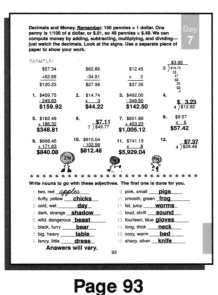

Write nouns to go with these adjectives. The first one is done for you.

1. two, red **apples**
2. fluffy, yellow **chicks**
3. cold, wet **day**
4. dark, strange **shadow**
5. wild, dangerous **beast**
6. black, furry **bear**
7. big, heavy **table**
8. fancy, little **dress**
9. pink, small **pigs**
10. smooth, green **frog**
11. fat, juicy **worms**
12. loud, shrill **sound**
13. fourteen, blue **gloves**
14. long, thick **neck**
15. cozy, warm **bed**
16. sharp, silver **knife**

Answers will vary.

93

Page 94

Add a prefix and a suffix to the following words; then choose five of the words and write a sentence with them.

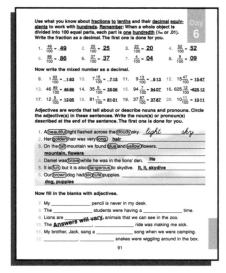

1. **un** lock **ed**
2. **de** light **ed**
3. **non** poison **ous**
4. **en** courage **ment**
5. **dis** agree **able**
6. **mis** spell **ed**
7. **un** print **ed**
8. **im** port **ant**
9. **pre** cook **ed**
10. **dis** appoint **ment**
11. **pre** record **ed**
12. **un** health **y**

Sentences:
1.
2.
3.
4.
5.

Sentences will vary.

What's for Breakfast, Lunch, and Dinner? This is your day to plan the meals. You can have anything you want to eat for the day. It can be for the whole family or just yourself. Plan and write down your menu for breakfast, lunch, and dinner. You can even schedule a few snacks.

Plan will vary.

94

Page 95

Multiplying Multiples of 10 and 100.
To use shortcuts to find the product of multiples of 10 or 100, write the product for the basic fact and count the zeros in the factors.
10 x 8 = 80 (1 zero)   10 x 80 = 800 (2 zeros)   10 x 800 = 8,000 (3 zeros)

Multiples of tens:

1. 10 x 5 = **50**
2. 7 x 10 = **70**
3. 39 x 10 = **390**
4. 30 x 30 = **900**
5. 54 x 10 = **540**
6. 10 x 21 = **210**
7. 710 x 10 = **7,100**
8. 9 x 10 = **90**
9. 70 x 30 = **2,100**
10. 40 x 40 = **1,600**
11. 85 x 10 = **850**
12. 341 x 10 = **3,410**

Multiples of hundreds:

13. 900 x 40 = **36,000**
14. 600 x 10 = **6,000**
15. 230 x 20 = **4,600**
16. 700 x 80 = **56,000**
17. 500 x 50 = **25,000**
18. 600 x 90 = **54,000**
19. 440 x 30 = **13,200**
20. 700 x 60 = **42,000**

Adjectives can be used to compare. Write these adjectives. Add -er and -est.

EXAMPLE: red   *redder*   *reddest*

1. hot   **hotter**   **hottest**
2. nice   **nicer**   **nicest**
3. warm   **warmer**   **warmest**
4. hard   **harder**   **hardest**
5. easy   **easier**   **easiest**
6. few   **fewer**   **fewest**

Now retell a Bible story. Use as many of the adjectives above as you can. Underline the adjectives.

Story will vary.

95

Page 96

Idioms. Choose 4 idioms and illustrate them. Here are some to choose from, or you can use your own.

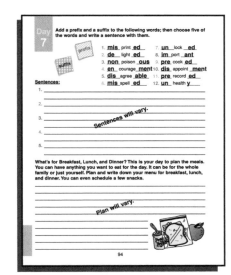

- Lend a hand.
- She's a ball of fire.
- He's got rocks in his head.
- She gave him a dirty look.
- I got it straight from the horse's mouth.
- You won the game by the skin of your teeth.
- Time flies.
- Keep a stiff upper lip.
- The boys were shooting the breeze.
- I'd really like to catch her eye.
- I was dog tired.

Pictures will vary.

96

Page 97

Place Value. A place-value chart can help us read as well as figure out large numbers.

Hundred Millions	Ten Millions	Millions	Hundred Thousands	Ten Thousands	Thousands	Hundreds	Tens	Ones
8	6	5	3	7	1	4	4	3

Using the place-value chart to help you, read and write the following numbers. The first one is done for you.

1. Eighty-six million five hundred thirty-seven thousand one hundred forty-three
   86,537,143
2. Seven hundred eighty-nine million four hundred ninety-six thousand three hundred twenty-one **789,496,321**
3. One hundred sixty million seven hundred six thousand one hundred twenty-nine
   160,706,129
4. Seventy-one million four hundred eleven thousand eight hundred ninety-nine
   71,411,899
5. One hundred million three hundred seventy-five thousand **100,375,000**
6. Ninety million two hundred fifty-seven thousand four hundred forty-three
   90,257,443
7. 1,369,000 _One million, three hundred sixty-nine thousand._
8. 375,403,101 _Three hundred seventy-five million, four hundred three thousand, one hundred one._
9. 894,336,045 _Eight hundred ninety-four million, three hundred thirty-six thousand, forty-five._
10. 284,300,070 _Two hundred eighty-four million, three hundred thousand, seventy._

Overworked And. Rewrite the paragraph and leave out all the occurrences of *and* that you can. Write in cursive *and* be sure to put capitals *and* periods where they need to go.

My friend and I visited Cardiff, Wales, and we learned that Cardiff is the capital and largest port of Wales and the city lies on the River Taff near the Bristol Channel and Cardiff is near the largest coal mines in Great Britain and it is one of the great coal-shipping ports of the world.

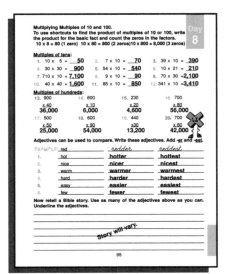

My friend and I visited Cardiff, Wales. We learned that Cardiff is the capital and largest port of Wales. The city lies on the River Taff near the Bristol Channel. Cardiff is near the largest coal mines in Great Britain. It is one of the great coal-shipping ports of the world.

How many times were you able to leave and out of the paragraph? **Four**

97

Page 98

Day 9

The following words are often misspelled. Write each word three times; then have someone give you a test. Use another piece of paper for your test.

EXAMPLE:

1. although — *although although although*
2. arithmetic — *arithmetic arithmetic arithmetic*
3. trouble — *trouble trouble trouble*
4. bought — *bought bought bought*
5. chocolate — *chocolate chocolate chocolate*
6. aunt — *aunt aunt aunt*
7. handkerchief — *handkerchief handkerchief handkerchief*
8. piece — *piece piece piece*
9. vacation — *vacation vacation vacation*
10. practice — *practice practice practice*
11. receive — *receive receive receive*
12. getting — *getting getting getting*
13. lessons — *lessons lessons lessons*
14. weather — *weather weather weather*
15. surprise — *surprise surprise surprise*

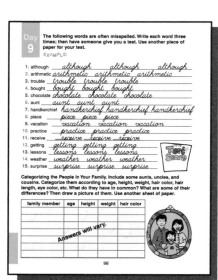

Categorizing the People in Your Family. Include some aunts, uncles, and cousins. Categorize them according to age, height, weight, hair color, hair length, eye color, etc. What do they have in common? What are some of their differences? Then draw a picture of them. Use another sheet of paper.

family member	age	height	weight	hair color

Answers will vary.

98

Page 99

Day 10

Multiplying 2-Digit Numbers.

1. 39 ×69 **2,691**	2. 72 ×18 **1,296**	3. 85 ×36 **3,060**
4. 46 ×77 **3,542**	5. 57 ×49 **2,793**	6. 41 ×73 **2,993**	7. 48 ×95 **4,560**	8. 88 ×66 **5,808**
9. 68 ×92 **6,256**	10. 507 ×13 **6,591**	11. 456 ×32 **14,592**	12. 640 ×21 **13,440**	13. 576 ×45 **25,920**

Write S behind the word pairs that are synonyms, A for antonyms, or H for homonyms.

EXAMPLE:

tie · bind **S**
high · low **A**
here · hear **H**

1. weep · cry **S**
2. wonderful · terrible **A**
3. look · glare **S**
4. huge · large **S**
5. away · toward **A**
6. walk · stroll **S**
7. never · always **A**
8. bear · bare **H**
9. ask · told **A**
10. cymbal · symbol **H**
11. many · numerous **S**
12. end · begin **A**
13. hair · hare **H**
14. move · transport **S**
15. problem · solution **A**
16. idea · thought **S**
17. claws · clause **H**
18. I'll · isle **H**
19. add · subtract **A**
20. try · attempt **S**
21. that · this **A**
22. doe · dough **H**
23. enough · ample **S**
24. board · bored **H**
25. day · date **S**
26. capital · capitol **H**
27. leave · arrive **A**

99

Page 100

Day 10

Do this crossword puzzle. Read the clues to help you decide what words go in the boxes.

Down
1. birds with webbed feet
2. plays the piano
3. gave money
4. holds up the gate
5. boards for building
6. frilly
11. do it again to a story
12. hair by the eye
13. carried Jesus at Passover

Across
2. red from the sun
5. won't bend easily
6. eat outside
8. beginning of a word
7. decay of food
10. very large; great
14. nothing in it
15. cook in

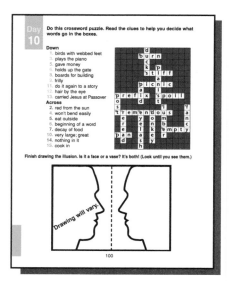

Finish drawing the illusion. Is it a face or a vase? It's both! (Look until you see them.)

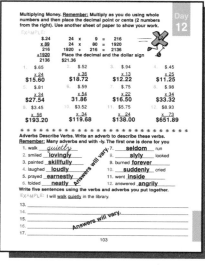

Drawing will vary.

100

Page 101

Day 11

Quotients with Remainders. Use another sheet of paper if you need to.

EXAMPLE:

1. 20)48 **2 R8**
2. 30)189 **6 R9**
3. 70)456 **6 R36**
4. 80)504 **6 R24**
5. 30)281 **9 R11**
6. 60)246 **4 R6**
7. 90)458 **5 R8**
8. 60)573 **9 R33**
9. 40)172 **4 R12**
10. 30)216 **7 R6**
11. 30)121 **4 R1**
12. 90)500 **5 R50**
13. 80)410 **5 R10**
14. 60)692 **11 R32**
15. 70)661 **9 R31**

Think of one of your favorite Bible stories. Tell how the story begins, what happens in the middle, and how it ends. Write it in your own words and in the correct order. Don't write the whole story.

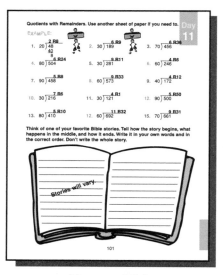

Stories will vary.

101

Page 102

Day 11

Categorize these words and tell why they go in the same category. You put the headings in this time.

Arrangement of answers may vary.

decillter, quart, anger, swimming, ounce, tennis, program, soccer, software, disk, Celsius, basketball, kindness, yard, jealousy, liter, mouse, rugby, remorse, hate, Fahrenheit, ton, cursor, kilogram, softball, acre, joystick, gram, meter, fear

1. Computer Words	2. Sports Words	3. Metric Words	4. Feeling Words	5. Standard Measurement
disk	swimming	meter	jealousy	ounce
cursor	tennis	liter	fear	quart
program	soccer	gram	kindness	ton
software	basketball	celsius	anger	fahrenheit
mouse	rugby	kilogram	remorse	acre
joystick	softball	decilliter	hate	yard

Tell why. Because they all...

1. _____
2. _____
3. _____
4. _____
5. _____

Answers will vary.

Make a "Happy" list and then a "Sad" list. Put the things that make you most happy at the top of your "Happy" list. Do the same thing with things that make you sad on your "Sad" list.

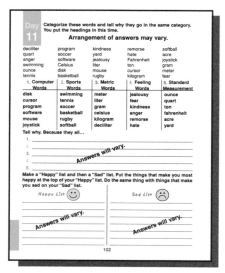

Happy List ☺   Sad List ☹

Answers will vary.   Answers will vary.

102

Page 103

Day 12

Multiplying Money. **Remember:** Multiply as you do using whole numbers and then place the decimal point or cents (2 numbers from the right). Use another sheet of paper to show your work.

EXAMPLE:

$.24
× 89
216
+1920
2136

24 × 9 = 216
24 × 80 = 1920
1920 + 216 = 2136
Place the decimal and the dollar sign
$21.36

1. $.65 ×24 **$15.60**	2. $.52 ×36 **$18.72**	3. $.94 ×13 **$12.22**	4. $.45 ×25 **$11.25**
5. $.81 ×34 **$27.54**	6. $.59 ×54 **31.86**	7. $.75 ×22 **$16.50**	8. $.98 ×34 **$33.32**
9. $3.45 ×56 **$193.20**	10. 3.52 ×34 **$119.68**	11. $5.75 ×24 **$138.00**	12. $8.93 ×73 **$651.89**

Adverbs Describe Verbs. Write an adverb to describe these verbs. **Remember:** Many adverbs end with -ly. The first one is done for you.

1. walk **quietly**
2. smiled **lovingly**
3. painted **skillfully**
4. laughed **loudly**
5. prayed **earnestly**
6. folded **neatly**
7. _____ **seldom** run
8. _____ **slyly** looked
9. burned **forever**
10. _____ **suddenly** cried
11. went **inside**
12. answered **angrily**

Answers will vary.

Write five sentences using the verbs and adverbs you put together.

EXAMPLE: I will walk quietly in the library.

13. _____
14. _____
15. _____
16. _____
17. _____

Answers will vary.

103

Page 104

Day 12

Read a book and fill out the following book report. Share it with a sister, brother, or friend.

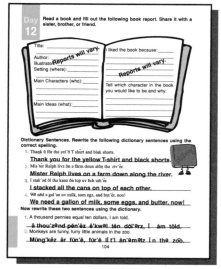

Title: _____
Author: _____
Illustrator: _____
Setting (where): _____
Main Characters (who): _____
Main Ideas (what): _____

I liked the book because: _____

Reports will vary.

Tell which character in the book you would like to be and why:

Dictionary Sentences. Rewrite the following dictionary sentences using the correct spelling.

1. Thang ū fôr tho yel'ō T shūrt and blak shorts.
   Thank you for the yellow T-shirt and black shorts.
2. Mis'ter Ralph līvz ŏn a fārm doun alŏng tha riv'ėr.
   Mister Ralph lives on a farm down along the river.
3. I stak'ed ôl tha kanz ŏn top uv ēch uth'ėr.
   I stacked all the cans on top of each other.
4. Wē nēd a gal'on uv milk, sum egz, and but'ėr, nou!
   We need a gallon of milk, some eggs, and butter, now!

Now rewrite these two sentences using the dictionary.

1. A thousand pennies equal ten dollars, I am told.
   ā thou'z'ånd pėn'ēz ē'kwėl tėn dŏl'ėrz, Ī ăm tōld.
2. Monkeys are funny, furry little animals in the zoo.
   Mŭng'kēz ār fŭn'ē, fûr'ē lit'l ăn'ėmėlz ĭn tha zōō.

104

Page 105

Day 13

Geometry. Explain to an adult what the following geometrical terms mean. Show what each means by drawing an example of each.

1. Segments, lines, endpoints, and rays
A segment is part of a line. A straight path from point A to point B is a segment. Sides of a polygon are segments. A line goes on and on in both directions. Lines and line segments are straight. A ray is part of a line, except it has one end-point.

2. Intersecting lines
Intersecting lines meet or intersect. E is the point of intersecting or meeting.

3. Parallel lines
Parallel lines run parallel to each other, having no points in common. They do not intersect at any point.

4. Perimeter
Perimeter is the distance around a figure or shape. 4 yds + 4 yds + 7 yds + 7 yds = 22 yds. This rectangle's perimeter is 22 yards.

Adverbs tell where, how, or when. Tell what kind of adverb is underlined in the following sentences. Write where, when, or how.

1. Animals are sometimes called mammals. **when**
2. There was a big accident on the freeway yesterday. **when**
3. Joe quickly ran out to catch the bus. **how**
4. We could hear the sound far below us. **where**
5. The wise men followed the brightly shining star. **how**
6. We are going there next winter. **where**
7. Be sure and write your letter neatly. **how**
8. The birds will fly away if you scare them. **where**
9. Father is going to leave immediately. **when**
10. The baby played happily on the lawn. **how**

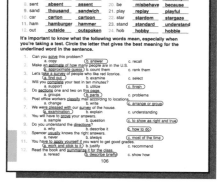

Where? How? When?

Now fill in the blanks with a how, when, or where adverb.

1. The car was going very (how) **fast**
2. Will you take April and June (where) **downtown** to the movie?
3. Mom will take them down (when) **later**

Answers will vary.

105

Page 106

Day 13

Add one or two syllables to the words below to make two new words. Make sure you spell the words correctly.

EXAMPLE: low **pillow**   follow

1. law **lawful** **lawless**
2. place **replace** **placement**
3. rock **rocket** **rocker**
4. tire **entire** **retired**
5. band **husband** **bandaid**
6. bat **battery** **battle**
7. bit **habit** **rabbit**
8. sent **absent** **assent**
9. sand **thousand** **sandwich**
10. car **carton** **cartoon**
11. ham **hamburger** **hammer**
12. out **outside** **outspoken**
13. able **syllable** **affordable**
14. age **cottage** **message**
15. ten **tenants** **attention**
16. man **woman** **mangle**
17. cat **cattle** **catch**
18. con **consonant** **reason**
19. con **bacon** **balcony**
20. be **misbehave** **misbehave**
21. play **replay** **playful**
22. star **stardom** **stargaze**
23. stand **standard** **understand**
24. hob **hobby** **hobble**

It's important to know what the following words mean, especially when you're taking a test. Circle the letter that gives the best meaning for the underlined word in the sentence.

1. Can you solve this problem?
   a. copy **b. answer** c. recall
2. Make an estimate of how many people are in the U.S.
   a. approximate guess b. count them c. rank them
3. Let's take a survey of people who like red licorice.
   a. find out b. examine c. select
4. Will you complete your test in ten minutes?
   a. support b. utilize **c. finish**
5. Do sections one and two on this page.
   a. groups **b. parts** c. problems
6. Post office workers classify mail according to locations.
   a. change b. write **c. arrange or group**
7. We were pleased with our survey of the house.
   a. examination b. explain c. describe it
8. You will have to prove your answers.
   a. sample b. question **c. to show as right and true**
9. Do you understand the directions?
   a. why b. describe it **c. how to do**
10. Spencer usually knows the right answers.
    a. never **b. most of the time** c. always
11. You have to apply yourself if you want to get good grades.
    a. work and stick to it b. justify c. recommend
12. Read the book and summarizing it for the class.
    a. reread **b. describe briefly** c. show how

106

124

Page 107

More Geometry. Explain and draw an example of the following geometrical terms.

1. Congruent figures are polygons that have the exact shape and size. The can be flipped, slid, or turned, but as long as they are the exact shape and size they are congruent.

   These are congruent figures.

2. Right angles are angles that form a square corner. All of these are right angles. When two lines form 4 right angles, we say that they are perpendicular.

   These are right angles.

3. Triangles have three sides and 3 vertices (vertex). Vertex is where the points meet.

4. Parallelograms are four-sided figures having the opposite sides parallel and equal.

5. Polygons are closed, straight sided figures. Triangles, hexagons, octagons, pentagons, and quadrilaterals are all polygons. This is also a polygon because it is a closed figure with straight lines.

   Sometimes it's fun to share a story with someone else. Read a book, then call one of your friends or go visit them. Tell your friend about the book you read.

   Tell who the main characters are. Tell where the story takes place. Tell the plot or main event of the story. But don't tell them how the story ends. See if you can get them to read the book.

   On the rest of this page, write what happened. Did you get your friend to read the book?

   Answers will vary.

   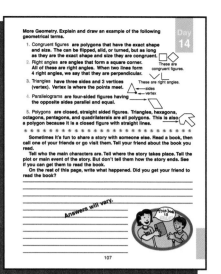

107

Page 108

Create small words from the letters in the following words. Write them. You may find more than one in most words.

EXAMPLE: borrow _sour_ _or_ _bour_ _rob_

1. pajamas **jam, am, as, a**
2. carpenter **car, pen, enter**
3. performance **perform, for, man**
4. bandage **band, and, age, ban, an**
5. knowledge **know, no, now, ledge**
6. theory **the, or, he**
7. satisfaction **sat, is, fact, act, at, action**
8. customer **us, Tom, custom**
9. discovery **is, cover, very**
10. eventually **even, all, vent**
11. announcement **an, no, men, cement, announce, noun, Ann, ounce**
12. creation **note, ten, ate, reaction, react, rate, cart, carton, acre**
13. theater **the, he, eat, ate**
14. honorable **honor, on, or, able**
15. investigate **in, vest, gate, ate, invest**

Sometimes things happen that cause something else to happen. This is called "cause and effect." A clue word helps to tell which is which. In the following sentences, underline the cause with a straight line (___). Underline the effect with a dotted line (_ _ _). Put a box ☐ around the clue word. The first one is done for you.

1. The tooth was broken, ☐so☐ it gave her a lot of pain.
2. The book was ripped and dirty ☐because☐ the dog got it.
3. ☐Because☐ it was so cold, Betty could ice skate for only a short while.
4. I went to bed early last night ☐because☐ I was so tired.
5. ☐Since☐ it was raining so hard, we couldn't play outside.
6. The rabbit ran fast ☐because☐ the fox was after it.
7. It was very foggy out, ☐so☐ we could not see the mountains.
8. ☐Because☐ we got to the camp late in the day, there was no time for hiking.
9. It was very dark in the dugout ☐so☐ we turned on the flashlight.
10. Kit played basketball too long after school; ☐therefore☐ he missed the bus.
11. Laura's letter was returned ☐because☐ she forgot to put a stamp on it.
12. Mike's suitcase broke when it fell off the car. ☐As a result☐ he had to put his things in a paper bag.

108

Page 109

Graphs, Charts, and Tables. There are many different kinds of graphs, charts, and tables. Check your newspaper regularly to find different kinds and different information that you could chart or graph daily. This is a "broken-line" graph. Complete this graph using the information given in the table. Monday and Tuesday have been done for you.

Day	Temperature
Monday	87°
Tuesday	90°
Wednesday	74°
Thursday	78°
Friday	80°

Highest Temperature

Write these sentences in the correct order. Underline the negative word in each sentence. The word that makes the sentence mean "no" or "not" is the negative word.

1. win won't contest I ever art an.

   I won't ever win an art contest.

2. involved does want be not He to.

   He does not want to be involved.

3. today I do have to no work more.

   I have no more work to do today.

4. nowhere play is us ball There for to.

   There is nowhere for us to play ball.

5. down never let will you God.

   God will never let you down.

6. ridden ever horse Jeremy a hasn't.

   Jeremy hasn't ever ridden a horse.

109

Page 110

Match the definitions below to a word in the Word Box. Find and circle the words in the puzzle. The first one has been done for you.

1. ABC order
2. not a vowel
3. more than one
4. names things
5. mark used for stress
6. part of a word
7. describes nouns
8. used in place of a noun
9. added to the beginning of a base word
10. just one
11. describes verbs
12. not a consonant
13. added to the end of a base word
14. shows action

Word Box

- ___ vowel
- ___ plural
- ___ syllable
- _1_ alphabetical
- ___ consonant
- ___ prefix
- ___ adjectives
- ___ nouns
- ___ verb
- ___ suffix
- ___ pronoun
- ___ adverbs
- ___ accent
- ___ singular

```
i z x a b u i o m e c f i t x z o c p r u t
u p r t v x o n i k b d f h j l i o m q s t
o o q s u i z a m j a c e g i k o n o u n s
j t s b r c i m s u f f i x b n o s r s t v
f d l v e r b i y q l i g h g a c o d f k l
b c u o x o k r l p u u i o t v e n e h i m
a a f w d z i a l p h a b e t i c a l i p m
p x c e g t l m a x q b c l l b c n j b o t
r u o l n p o k b a d g j t o t f l u a i i
y a d v e r b s l c l i l o p r e f i x l e
k d x f g j k l b e h k i r b f g o e n e l
m j z h i o q a r v x y z a o a c c e n t o
l e c m o n p t u i w e a i n w x y z a b c
a c d w e f h j i m n o q r o n o x y z e l
p t e a b e m o e g h i e p l u r a l i m o t
s i n g u l a r f j k n i o n e a k l u p x
y v c d e a d e j m v y z i t m l o x z b a
o e b f g k n o q s w f o u l n a d g i m n
e c h i l p r t y x b c e f h k l o r s t
```

110

Vacation Bible Camp

A special note to parents about Vacation Bible Camp

As your child completes the activities in this book to maintain important academic skills, it is also vital for your child to further develop spiritual skills. That's why we've created this special bonus section. You and your child may have noticed a theme in the daily devotions. The verses and quotes chosen were based on characteristics of Biblical heroes: courage, faith, strength, confidence, and hope. These heroic characteristics are the foundation for this bonus section, which contains 10 weekly lessons based on heroes of the Bible. Two pages of activities are dedicated to each Vacation Bible Camp lesson. On the first page you'll find activities for days 1–3 for the week: the scripture reference containing the Bible hero's story, a related memory verse, and everyday application questions. The second page has activities for days 4 and 5: a craft and a journal-writing reflection.

There are many stories in the Bible of people who acted heroically by accomplishing amazing feats of strength, such as the well-known story of young David defeating Goliath. But being a hero takes more than physical strength. It also requires courage, faith, confidence, hope, and internal strength—all of which come from the Lord. It is difficult to select just 10 heroes from the Bible. The 10 we chose for Vacation Bible Camp are people of varying backgrounds and abilities who became heroic examples to us all. Some of them accomplished miraculous achievements, while others serve as powerful reminders that a hero is a person who makes a positive difference in the lives of others. The Bible heroes you and your child will learn about in this section are Miriam, Samuel, Esther, Daniel, Rahab, Elisha, Mary Magdalene, Paul, Mary, and Jesus. Children need to understand that heroes are not things of the past, but that they, too, can be everyday heroes by using the gifts that God gave them to help others.

It is important for you to complete the lessons with your child so you can assist him or her in finding the complete value in each lesson. All five of the week's activities coordinate and build on one another. Start day 1 by reading the Bible lesson straight from scripture; then help your child describe how the hero acted heroically. On day 2, discuss and help your child memorize the Bible verse. On day 3, answer the everyday application questions together. By day 4, your child should be picking up on the overall theme of the lesson as you prepare the craft. On day 5, complete the lesson with the journal reflection so that your child can "become the hero."

Before each week's lesson, review the activities to ensure that you have all the needed supplies, since many of the crafts require some basic craft materials. Again, adult supervision is strongly encouraged as your child completes the 10 weeks of Vacation Bible Camp, both because it helps you and your child to get the most from the lessons and because some of the activities themselves, such as baking in the oven, require an adult.

You'll likely have as much fun attending Vacation Bible Camp as your child will—and you may even learn something!

Vacation Bible Camp

When you've completed the 10 weeks of Vacation Bible Camp, take some time to reflect on what you have learned.

1. What was the most fun activity you completed? _____

   _____

   _____

2. What was the hardest activity you completed? _____

   _____

   _____

3. What did you like best about Vacation Bible Camp? _____

   _____

   _____

4. What was the most important thing you learned? _____

   _____

   _____

5. What can you share with others about what you learned? _____

   _____

   _____

Vacation Bible Camp

Week 1—Miriam

Day 1—Bible Hero Background

> **Scripture** Read **Exodus 2:1–10**
> for the biblical account of Miriam's heroic actions.

Describe how Moses' sister Miriam acted heroically in this Bible story.

Day 2—Related Memory Verse

Read and memorize the verse.

> **Psalm 112:7**
> He will have no fear of bad news;
> his heart is steadfast, trusting in the LORD.

How does this verse remind you of Miriam?

Day 3—Everyday Application

Think about Miriam and yourself; then answer the following questions.

What lesson can be learned from Miriam?

What character trait best describes Miriam?

What can you do to be like Miriam?

Vacation Bible Camp

Day 4—Craft—Woven Basket

Baby Moses was placed in a basket and watched over by Miriam. Make this woven basket as a reminder of how you are kept safe under the watchful eye of the Lord.

Materials Needed:

clean plastic container (such as a large margarine tub)
2 skeins of yarn (2 different colors)
scissors
felt
glue

Assembly:

Have an adult help you cut 1/2-inch strips down the sides of the plastic container. Pick the first color of yarn for the bottom of the basket. Start the yarn between two of the strips and weave it in and out of each strip and around the basket, going from left to right or right to left. As each row is finished, push it down against to the row below it. Keep the yarn tight as you wind it around the container, but not so tight that it pulls the sides of the container into the center. Weave the yarn around the strips until you have covered the bottom half of the container. Switch to the other color of yarn by tying one end to the old color. Repeat the weaving process until the container is covered to the top. Trim off the yarn and glue down the ends. Cut out a felt center piece to fit the bottom of the container and glue it to the inside of the container. Make a yarn braid and glue it on either side of the upper insides of the basket's brim. Allow to dry.

Day 5—Become the Hero

What do you think Miriam was thinking when the servant was about to take baby Moses away?

How do you think she was able to overcome her fear and think quickly?

Vacation Bible Camp
Week 2—Samuel

Day 1—Bible Hero Background

> **Scripture** Read **1 Samuel 3**
> for the biblical account of Samuel's heroic actions.

Describe how Samuel acted heroically in this Bible story.

Day 2—Related Memory Verse

Read and memorize the verse.

> **Proverbs 16:13**
> Kings take pleasure in honest lips;
> they value a man who speaks the truth

How does this verse remind you of Samuel?

Day 3—Everyday Application

Think about Samuel and yourself; then answer the following questions:

What character trait best describes Samuel?

What can you do to be like Samuel?

Vacation Bible Camp

Day 4—Craft—Lamp

Each time Samuel came to Eli's side, the lamp of God was there to guide his way. Make your own lamp as a symbol of how God is always there to lead you.

Materials Needed:

self-hardening clay
craft paints
craft paintbrushes
sequins
glue

varnish (optional)
tea light candle

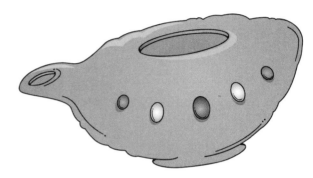

Assembly:

Using a ball of clay about three inches in diameter, roll the ball into a long sausage shape about 1/4 inch thick. Form the base of the lamp by curling the clay around on itself to form a flat spiral shape about two inches in diameter. Build up the sides of the lamp by curling more clay coils around until a small pot about one inch high is formed. Taper off the end of the clay to form a level edge. Using your finger and a little water, smooth the coils together to form a smooth outer surface. With your thumb and forefinger, gently pinch one side of the pot at the top and pull slightly outwards to form a spout. Smooth again and then allow to dry. When the lamp is dry, paint it inside and out. Allow to dry. Glue sequins on the outside of the lamp for decoration. For a more permanent finish, apply varnish to the lamp. Once decorated, place a tea light candle inside the lamp. Only use the lamp under adult supervision.

Day 5—Become the Hero

What do you think Samuel was thinking when he realized that the Lord was calling him?

How do you think he was able to have the courage to be honest with Eli?

Vacation Bible Camp

Week 3—Esther

Day 1—Bible Hero Background

> **Scripture** Read **Esther 3:19–52**
> for the biblical account of Esther's heroic actions.

Describe how Esther acted heroically in this Bible story.

Day 2—Related Memory Verse

Read and memorize the verse.

> **Isaiah 41:13**
> For I am the LORD, your God, who takes
> hold of your right hand and says to you,
> Do not fear; I will help you.

How does this verse remind you of Esther?

Day 3—Everyday Application

Think about Esther and yourself; then answer the following questions:

I was a hero like Esther when...

What lesson can be learned from Esther?

What character trait best describes Esther?

Vacation Bible Camp

Day 4—Craft—Crown

The king approved of Esther and made her a queen, able to wear a royal crown, but the more valuable gift she wore was God's love and protection. Make a "jeweled" crown to represent how the Lord is with you at all times.

Materials Needed:

newspapers

cereal box (separated at the seams and flattened)

scissors

markers

stapler

glitter glue pens

Assembly:

Cut a length of the cereal box approximately six inches wide and long enough to go around your head and overlap slightly at the ends. Cut a jagged or scalloped design around the top edge. Use glitter glue pens to draw outlines of jewel shapes such as diamonds and ovals. In each jewel shape write a word, short phrase, or verse reference about God's love and protection. Staple the overlapping ends together.

Day 5—Become the Hero

What do you think Esther was thinking when she was walking toward the king?

How do you think she was able to have the inner strength to approach him?

Vacation Bible Camp

Week 4—Elisha

Day 1—Bible Hero Background

> **Scripture** Read **1 Kings 19:19–21**
> for the biblical account of Elisha's heroic actions.

Describe how Elisha acted heroically in this Bible story.

Day 2—Related Memory Verse

Read and memorize the verse.

> **Luke 12:15** Then he said to them,
> "Watch out! Be on your guard against all kinds of
> greed; a man's life does not consist in the abundance
> of his possessions."

How does this verse remind you of Elisha?

Day 3—Everyday Application

Think about Elisha and yourself; then answer the following questions:

How are you like Elisha?

What character trait best describes Elisha?

What lesson can be learned from Elisha?

Vacation Bible Camp

Day 4—Craft—Heaven Scrapbook

When Elijah called Elisha to follow God, Elisha wanted to go back and say good-bye to his parents first. He was thinking more about his past than he was about his future, which included eternity in heaven! Make a scrapbook of heaven showing things that those who trust in Christ have to look forward to.

Materials Needed:

hole punch	scissors	stickers (optional)
fabric remnants or	markers	glitter glue pens
wrapping paper	glue	(optional)
construction paper	magazines	
empty cereal box	yarn or ribbon	

Assembly:

Cut the front and back panels from the cereal box to make the front and back covers of the scrapbook. Glue a fabric remnant or wrapping paper over each panel, front and back. Use the hole punch to make three holes along the left side of the front and back cover and three holes along the left side of seven sheets of construction paper, which will be used as the inside scrapbook pages. Assemble the scrapbook by lining up the holes and securing each set of holes with a length of yarn or ribbon. Label each page with a title, such as "My Family." On each scrapbook page, add pictures cut from magazines or drawn by hand that represent what heaven will be like. Enhance each page by adding stickers or glitter glue designs. To complete the project, use marker or glitter glue to embellish the cover by adding a title, such as "Heaven: My Future Home."

Day 5—Become the Hero

What do you think Elisha was thinking when he was told he had to leave his family behind?

How do you think he was able to trust Elijah and follow God's calling?

Vacation Bible Camp

Week 5—Rahab

Day 1—Bible Hero Background

> **Scripture** Read **Joshua 2**
> for the biblical account of Rahab's heroic actions.

Describe how Rahab acted heroically in this Bible story.

Day 2—Related Memory Verse

Read and memorize the verse.

> **Deuteronomy 4:39**
> Acknowledge and take to heart this day
> that the LORD is God in heaven above
> and on the earth below. There is no other.

How does this verse remind you of Rahab?

Day 3—Everyday Application

Think about Rahab and yourself; then answer the following questions:

What lesson can be learned from Rahab?

What character trait best describes Rahab?

What can you do to be like Rahab?

Vacation Bible Camp

Day 4—Craft—Scarlet Cord Bookmark

Rahab was instructed to hang a scarlet cord from her window as a sign to the spies. Because of her faithfulness to and recognition of God, her life and her family were spared. Make a special bookmark to serve as a reminder of how important it is to acknowledge our awesome God.

Materials Needed:

card stock
scissors
single hole punch
markers
stickers or glitter glue

clear contact paper
red macramé cord or
     thick red ribbon

Assembly:

Cut out the card stock into a long rectangle, approximately 2" x 8". Neatly write a Bible verse about recognizing God's power, such as Deuteronomy 4:39. Highlight the written verse with stickers or glitter glue designs. Cover the bookmark with clear contact paper. Punch a hole at the top of the bookmark and thread the cord or ribbon through the hole to form a tassel.

Day 5—Become the Hero

What do you think Rahab was thinking when she was hiding the spies?

How do you think she was able to stand confidently before the king's men who were looking for the spies?

Vacation Bible Camp
Week 6—Daniel

Day 1—Bible Hero Background

> Scripture Read **Daniel 5**
> for the biblical account of Daniel's heroic actions.

Describe how Daniel acted heroically in this Bible story.

Day 2—Related Memory Verse

Read and memorize the verse.

> **1 Timothy 6:17** Command those who are rich in this present world not to be arrogant nor to put their hope in wealth, which is so uncertain, but to put their hope in God, who richly provides us with everything for our enjoyment.

How does this verse remind you of Daniel?

Day 3—Everyday Application

Think about Daniel and yourself; then answer the following questions:

I was a hero like Daniel when...

What lesson can be learned from Daniel?

What character trait best describes Daniel?

Vacation Bible Camp

Day 4—Craft—Mystery Code

Daniel consistently used his God-given gifts to serve the Lord's purpose, including interpreting the mysterious writing on the wall. Make your own important hidden message from God using "invisible ink" and the scriptures.

Materials Needed:

lemon juice
small bowl
cotton swab
white copy paper
(8 1/2" x 11")

glue
construction paper
(10" x 12 1/2")

Assembly:

Pour two teaspoons of lemon juice into a bowl. Dip a cotton swab into the lemon juice. On a piece of white copy paper, use the dipped end of the cotton swab to write down a Bible verse about God giving us gifts and talents. When the writing has dried, give the paper to someone. Instruct the person to hold the paper next to a lightbulb so the unreadable message will become clear. After the message has been read, glue the paper onto a larger piece of construction paper to frame it and display the message as a reminder of Daniel's heroic example.

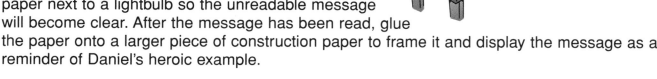

Day 5—Become the Hero

What do you think Daniel was thinking when he was brought before the king?

How do you think he was able to so easily turn down the riches the king offered him?

Vacation Bible Camp

Week 7—Mary Magdalene

Day 1—Bible Hero Background

Scripture Read **John 20:10–18** for the biblical account of Mary Magdalene's heroic actions.

Describe how Mary Magdalene acted heroically in this Bible story.

Day 2—Related Memory Verse

Read and memorize the verse.

Mark 11:23 "I tell you the truth, if anyone says to this mountain, 'Go, throw yourself into the sea,' and does not doubt in his heart but believes that what he says will happen, it will be done for him."

How does this verse remind you of Mary Magdalene?

Day 3—Everyday Application

Think about Mary Magdalene and yourself; then answer the following questions:

What lesson can be learned from Mary Magdalene?

What character trait best describes Mary Magdalene?

What can you do to be like Mary Magdalene?

Vacation Bible Camp

Day 4—Craft—Clay Pendant Necklaces

Mary Magdalene shared the good news of Christ's resurrection without hesitation. Make necklaces to serve as reminders that we should be ready to share the story of Jesus's love and sacrifice.

Materials Needed:

modeling dough (see recipe to follow)	glitter glue pens
craft paints	permanent black marker
paintbrushes	yarn or ribbon

Modeling Dough Ingredients:

2 cups baking soda	waxed paper
1 1/4 cups water	round cookie cutter
1 cup cornstarch	toothpick
rolling pin	

Assembly:

Prepare the modeling dough by combining the baking soda and cornstarch. Add the water. Mix thoroughly in a sauce pan and stir over medium heat until mixture comes to a low boil. Continue until a dough consistency is reached. Turn the dough onto a plate covered with a damp cloth. Refrigerate for half an hour. Knead the dough for 3-4 minutes. Flour the waxed paper. Roll the dough 1/4-inch thick. Cut with the round cookie cutter to make circular pendant shapes. Make a hole in the top of each circle with a toothpick. Let the dough circles dry for several hours. Have an adult heat the oven to 350 degrees. Place the circles onto a cookie sheet, and have an adult put the cookie sheet in the oven. When the tops of the circles appear dry (a few minutes) turn each over with a spatula and dry the backs. When the circles have cooled, paint each one a bright color. Decorate each circle's edge with glitter glue. In the center of each circle, write a verse or statement about the good news of Christ's death and resurrection. String a long length of yarn or ribbon through the hole in each circle to complete each necklace. Wear one of the necklaces yourself, and give the others to friends and family members who want to share the news of Christ, too.

Day 5—Become the Hero

What do you think Mary Magdalene was thinking when she realized that Jesus was alive and standing before her?

How do you think she was able to confidently tell the disciples that she had just spoken to Jesus?

Vacation Bible Camp

Week 8—Paul

Day 1—Bible Hero Background

> **Scripture** Read **Acts 27**
> for the biblical account of Paul's heroic actions.

Describe how Paul acted heroically in this Bible story.

Day 2—Related Memory Verse

Read and memorize the verse.

> **Hebrews 11:1**
> Now faith is being sure of what we hope for and
> certain of what we do not see.

How does this verse remind you of Paul?

Day 3—Everyday Application

Think about Paul and yourself; then answer the following questions.

How are you like Paul?

I was a hero like Paul when...

What character trait best describes Paul?

Vacation Bible Camp

Day 4—Craft—Shoe Box Ship Diorama

Paul had faith in what God had told him and had no doubts. Make a diorama to show the exciting ship scene described in Acts 27.

Materials Needed:

construction paper
shoe box
markers
glue
scissors
sticky-tack
yarn scraps
  (for outlined objects)
fabric scraps
  (for clothes and flat objects)

chenille craft stems (for
  seaweed and tree trunks)
glitter
  (for bubbles and waves)
thin cardboard
  (for large, shaped objects)
plastic ocean
  animals (optional)

Assembly:

Decide which aspect of the scene to show—fighting the stormy sea or wrecked on land. Build the diorama by working from the back to the front. Make the background first using construction paper. Remember to create the sky and ground or ocean.

With the various craft materials, make each of the props that need to be included in the scene, such as people and the ship. Place large objects towards the back of the box and smaller objects near the front. Use glue or sticky-tack to secure the objects in place.

Day 5—Become the Hero

What do you think Paul was thinking when the storm began?

How do you think he was able to have such hope that he would be safe?

Vacation Bible Camp

Week 9—Mary

Day 1—Bible Hero Background

> **Scripture** Read **Luke 1:26–55**
> for the biblical account of Mary's heroic actions.

Describe how Mary acted heroically in this Bible story.

Day 2—Related Memory Verse

Read and memorize the verse.

> **1 Peter 5:6**
> Humble yourselves, therefore, under God's mighty
> hand, that he may lift you up in due time.

How does this verse remind you of Mary?

Day 3—Everyday Application

Think about Mary and yourself; then answer the following questions.

What lesson can be learned from Mary?

What character trait best describes Mary?

What can you do to be like Mary?

Vacation Bible Camp

Day 4—Craft—Framed Mary's Song

When Mary learned that she was pregnant with Jesus, she responded with a humble spirit. Make a special frame to hold Mary's beautiful song of celebration from Luke 1:46–55.

Materials Needed:

computer
white paper
5" x 7" piece of cardboard
craft paint
foam paintbrush
fine-tipped marker
glue

glitter glue pens (optional)
stickers (optional)
sequins (optional)
plastic beads (optional)
craft knife
ribbon or magnet strip

Assembly:

Type the verses from Luke 1:46–55 and print them out using an attractive font. Leaving about half an inch of white space around the verses, cut off the excess paper. Center the paper on top of the piece of cardboard and lightly trace around it. Have an adult use a craft knife to cut out a hole for the verse, making sure to cut at least a quarter of an inch inside the lines to leave enough of a cardboard lip around the hole to glue the paper in place. Paint the front of the cardboard frame. Glue various craft accents to the frame. Glue the paper in place on the back side of the frame. Attach ribbon or a magnet strip to the back to display.

> **Mary's Song**
>
> "My soul glorifies the Lord
> and my spirit rejoices in God my Savior,
> for he has been mindful
> of the humble state of his servant.
> From now on all generations will call me blessed,
> for the Mighty One has done great things for me?
> holy is his name.
> His mercy extends to those who fear him,
> from generation to generation.
> He has performed mighty deeds with his arm;
> he has scattered those who are proud in
> their inmost thoughts.
> He has brought down rulers from their thrones
> but has lifted up the humble.
> He has filled the hungry with good things
> but has sent the rich away empty.
> He has helped his servant Israel,
> remembering to be merciful
> to Abraham and his descendants forever,
> even as he said to our fathers."
>
> Luke 1:46–55

Day 5—Become the Hero

What do you think Mary was thinking when the angel told her she was going to have a child?

How do you think she was able to maintain her faith after hearing the angel's amazing message?

Vacation Bible Camp

Week 10—Jesus

Day 1—Bible Hero Background

> **Scripture** Read **Matthew 28:1–10**
> for the biblical account of Jesus' heroic actions.

Describe how Jesus committed the ultimate heroic act in this Bible story.

Day 2—Related Memory Verse

Read and memorize the verse.

> **John 3:16**
> For God so loved the world that he gave
> his one and only Son, that whoever believes in him
> shall not perish but have eternal life.

How does this verse make you feel?

Day 3—Everyday Application

Think about Jesus and yourself; then answer the following questions.

How can you share the story of Jesus with others?

I can strive to be more Christlike each day by...

What is the most important lesson that can be learned from the life of Jesus?

What can you do today to be like Jesus?

Vacation Bible Camp

Day 4—Craft—Resurrection T-shirt

Jesus is the ultimate hero! Make a T-shirt that shares the importance of remembering and appreciating Jesus' love and sacrifice.

Materials Needed:

plain, light-colored T-shirt
fabric markers or permanent markers

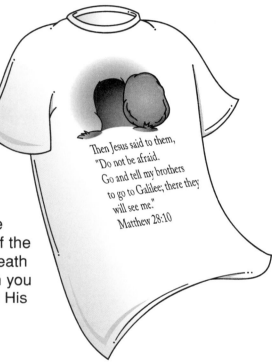

Then Jesus said to them, "Do not be afraid. Go and tell my brothers to go to Galilee; there they will see me." Matthew 28:10

Assembly:

Lay out the T-shirt on a flat surface. Write a verse that is special to you along each sleeve edge. On the front of the shirt, draw a design that represents Christ. On the back of the shirt, write a Bible verse or short passage about Jesus' death and resurrection. Add additional designs, if desired. When you wear the T-shirt, be ready to share the story of Jesus and His love for each and every one of us!

Day 5—Become the Hero

What do you think is the best way to share the heroic story of Jesus' love?

How can you be an everyday hero and make a difference in the lives of others?

Multiplication and Division

Developing multiplication and division math skills can be a challenging experience for both parent and child.

- **Have a positive attitude.**
- **Relax and enjoy the learning process.**
- **Keep the learning time short and fun you will get better results.**
- **Review the cards with your child.**
- **Read the front of the card.**
- **Check your answer on the reverse side.**
- **Separate those he/she does not know.**
- **Review those he/she does know.**
- **Gradually work through the other cards.**

These steps will help build your child's confidence with multiplication and division. Enjoy the rewards!

"Teacher, Teacher"

Three or more players.
Each player takes a turn as "Teacher."
The Teacher mixes up the flashcards and holds one card up at a time.
First player to yell out "Teacher, Teacher,"
will have the first chance to give the answer.
If his/her answer is right he/she receives 5 points.
If his/her answer is wrong, he/she will not receive any points.
Move on to the next person until someone answers correctly.
The next round someone else is teacher.
Repeat each round.
Reward the different levels, everyone wins!

Time Challenge

Follow the directions for "Teacher, Teacher" and add a time to it.
Increase the point system to meet the Time Challenge.
Reward the different levels, everyone wins!

0 x 0 4	0 x 1 3	0 x 2 2	0 x 3 1
0 x 4 8	0 x 5 7	0 x 6 6	0 x 7 5
0 x 8 3	0 x 9 2	0 x 10 1	1 x 1 9

$1\overline{)1}$

0

$1\overline{)2}$

0

$1\overline{)3}$

0

$1\overline{)4}$

0

$1\overline{)5}$

0

$1\overline{)6}$

0

$1\overline{)7}$

0

$1\overline{)8}$

0

$1\overline{)9}$

1

$2\overline{)2}$

0

$2\overline{)4}$

0

$2\overline{)6}$

0

2 x 1	2 x 2	3 x 1	3 x 2
7	6	5	4
3 x 3	4 x 1	4 x 2	4 x 3
2	1	9	8
4 x 4	5 x 1	5 x 2	5 x 3
6	5	4	3

$2\overline{)8}$

$2\overline{)10}$

$2\overline{)12}$

$2\overline{)14}$

6

3

4

2

$2\overline{)16}$

$2\overline{)18}$

$3\overline{)3}$

$3\overline{)6}$

12

8

4

9

$3\overline{)9}$

$3\overline{)12}$

$3\overline{)15}$

$3\overline{)18}$

15

10

5

16

5 x 4 1	5 x 5 9	6 x 1 8	6 x 2 7
6 x 3 5	6 x 4 4	6 x 5 3	6 x 6 2
7 x 1 9	7 x 2 8	7 x 3 7	7 x 4 6

$3 \overline{)21}$

12

$3 \overline{)24}$

6

$3 \overline{)27}$

25

$4 \overline{)4}$

20

$4 \overline{)8}$

36

$4 \overline{)12}$

30

$4 \overline{)16}$

24

$4 \overline{)20}$

18

$4 \overline{)24}$

28

$4 \overline{)28}$

21

$4 \overline{)32}$

14

$4 \overline{)36}$

7

7	7	7	8
x 5	x 6	x 7	x 1
4	3	2	1

8	8	8	8
x 2	x 3	x 4	x 5
8	7	6	5

8	8	8	9
x 6	x 7	x 8	x 1
3	2	1	9

5)‾5	5)‾10	5)‾15	5)‾20
8	49	42	35
5)‾25	5)‾30	5)‾35	5)‾40
40	32	24	16
5)‾45	6)‾6	6)‾12	6)‾18
9	64	56	48

9 x 2 7	9 x 3 6	9 x 4 5	9 x 5 4
9 x 6 2	9 x 7 1	9 x 8 9	9 x 9 8
10 x 1 6	10 x 2 5	10 x 3 4	10 x 4 3

6)24	6)30	6)36	6)42
45	36	27	18
6)48	6)54	7)7	7)14
81	72	63	54
7)21	7)28	7)35	7)42
40	30	20	10

10 × 5 7	10 × 6 6	10 × 7 5	10 × 8 4
10 × 9 2	10 ×10 1	7)49 9	7)56 8
7)63 6	8)8 5	8)16 4	8)24 3

$8\overline{)32}$

80

$8\overline{)40}$

70

$8\overline{)48}$

60

$8\overline{)56}$

50

$8\overline{)64}$

8

$8\overline{)72}$

7

$9\overline{)9}$

100

$9\overline{)18}$

90

$9\overline{)27}$

3

$9\overline{)36}$

2

$9\overline{)45}$

1

$9\overline{)54}$

9

$9\overline{)63}$	$9\overline{)72}$	$9\overline{)81}$	$10\overline{)10}$
$10\overline{)20}$	$10\overline{)30}$	$10\overline{)40}$	$10\overline{)50}$
$10\overline{)60}$	$10\overline{)70}$	$10\overline{)80}$	$10\overline{)90}$

$1 \overline{)0}$

$2 \overline{)0}$

$3 \overline{)0}$

$4 \overline{)0}$

$5 \overline{)0}$

$6 \overline{)0}$

$7 \overline{)0}$

$8 \overline{)0}$

$9 \overline{)0}$

$10 \overline{)0}$

Congratulations!

You

Your Name

have completed

Summer Bridge Activities™ *for Young Christians*

Miss Hansen's Signature

Ms. Hansen

Mr. Fredrickson's Signature

M. Fredrickson

Parent's Signature

God is love.

God is love.